How to Read Like You Mean It

Cultural Dialectics

The difference between subject and object slices through subject as well as through object.

—Theodor W. Adorno

Cultural Dialectics provides an open arena in which to debate questions of culture and dialectic—their practices, their theoretical forms, and their relations to one another and to other spheres and modes of inquiry. Approaches that draw on any of the following are especially encouraged: continental philosophy, psychoanalysis, the Frankfurt and Birmingham schools of cultural theory, deconstruction, gender theory, postcoloniality, and interdisciplinarity.

Series Titles

Northern Love: An Exploration of Canadian Masculinity
Paul Nonnekes

Making Game: An Essay on Hunting, Familiar Things, and the Strangeness of Being Who One Is
Peter L. Atkinson

Valences of Interdisciplinarity: Theory, Pedagogy, Practice
Edited by Raphael Foshay

Imperfection
Patrick Grant

The Undiscovered Country: Essays in Canadian Intellectual Culture
Ian Angus

The Letters of Vincent van Gogh: A Critical Study
Patrick Grant

"My Own Portrait in Writing": Self-Fashioning in the Letters of Vincent van Gogh
Patrick Grant

Speaking Power to Truth: Digital Discourse and the Public Intellectual
Edited by Michael Keren and Richard Hawkins

The Digital Nexus: Identity, Agency, and Political Engagement
Edited by Raphael Foshay

How to Read Like You Mean It
Kyle Conway

How to Read Like You Mean It

KYLE CONWAY

◊ AU PRESS

Published by AU Press, Athabasca University
1 University Drive, Athabasca, AB T9S 3A3
https://doi.org/10.15215/aupress/9781771993746.01

Cover design by Natalie Olsen, kisscutdesign.com
Printed and bound in Canada

Library and Archives Canada Cataloguing in Publication

Title: How to read like you mean it / Kyle Conway.
Names: Conway, Kyle, 1977– author.
Series: Cultural dialectics.
Description: Series statement: Cultural dialectics | Includes bibliographical
      references and index.
Identifiers: Canadiana (print) 20230207227 | Canadiana (ebook) 20230207332 |
      ISBN 9781771993746 (softcover) | ISBN 9781771993753 (PDF) |
      ISBN 9781771993760 (EPUB)
Subjects: LCSH: Reading comprehension. | LCSH: Uncertainty. |
      LCSH: Hermeneutics.
Classification: LCC LB1050.45 .C66 2023 | DDC 372.47—dc23

We acknowledge the financial support of the Government of Canada through
the Canada Book Fund (CBF) for our publishing activities and the assistance
provided by the Government of Alberta through the Alberta Media Fund.

Canada   Alberta
                  Government

For B. and E., the points on my compass
For K., world-changer

In memoriam Dad

Contents

List of Figures and Tables *ix*

Preface: How to Read This Book *xi*

Acknowledgements *xv*

Introduction: What Is Reading? *3*

1 To Read Is to Feel Lost *29*

2 To Read Is to Wander *55*

3 To Read Is to Feel Love *83*

4 To Read Is to Be Free *107*

Conclusion: To Read Is to Live with Other People *133*

References *153*

Index *163*

Figures and Tables

Figures

Figure 1   How is a raven like a writing desk? What trait connects them?   16

Figure 2   Certainty as a term linking different rates at which strangers ask questions   24

Figure 3   "Jargon has become the emperor's clothing of choice."   40

Figure 4   A hapless pilot, falling into the void   45

Figure 5   Dialectic relationship between objective and subjective dimensions of interpretation   63

Figure 6   Relation of the parts to the whole in Ricoeur's work on metaphor   68

Figure 7   Intertextual associations evoked by Ricoeur in his discussion of probability   69

Figure 8   Interpreting the pandemic through the process of guessing and validation   74

Figure 9   The vital force of eros, like a plant reaching up toward the sun   89

Figure 10   Sappho's narrator spies the woman she loves   95

Figure 11   A text, like a door, pushing back as a reader pushes against it   111

Figure 12   Inquiry's first step: what can we observe?   116

Figure 13   Inquiry's second step: what does the evidence reveal?   117

Figure 14   The recursive mode of inquiry as a hermeneutic circle   121

Figure 15   A mural depicting Picasso's painting *Guernica*   141

Figure 16   A door through which we might enter the world of another person   145

Tables

Table 1   The values, goals, and warrants of the discovery, interpretive, and critical paradigms   13

Table 2   Metaphor, text, and meaningful action as forms of discourse   35

Table 3   Strategies for guessing and criteria for validation   67

Table 4   Reproducibility and persuasiveness as competing conceptions of rigour   114

Table 5   What scholars within the persuasiveness paradigm learn by borrowing from the reproducibility paradigm   127

Table 6   What researchers within the reproducibility paradigm learn by borrowing from the persuasiveness paradigm   129

Table 7   Ontological vehemence at the level of metaphor, text, and meaningful action   137

Preface

How to Read This Book

———•———

At its most basic, this is a book about how to read difficult texts, and I am addressing it like a letter to my students. As I write in the introduction, it picks up where an earlier book left off; that book, too, I addressed like a letter to my students.[1] In both cases, I have drawn inspiration from the poet Roque Dalton, who wrote, "I believe the world is beautiful / and that poetry, like bread, is for everyone."[2] I agree about poetry (it pervades this book), but I'll go further. The joy of discovering new worlds through difficult texts (in other words, the joy of reading), like bread, is for everyone.

This strategy has influenced my choices related to style and, by way of style, my mode of argumentation. I am following a precept set forth by Paul Ricoeur, who emerges as the hero of this book, if academic books can be said to have heroes. Ricoeur explained in a 1988 interview that writers face a choice between "writing for the general public" and "writing for the greatest specialist in one's discipline, the one you have to convince."[3] He also said, "we must describe the complex object, but intervene where we are."[4] I am writing for my students, who are much closer to the general public than disciplinary

---

1 Kyle Conway, *The Art of Communication in a Polarized World.*
2 Roque Dalton, "Like You."
3 Paul Ricoeur, *Philosophy, Ethics, and Politics,* 5.
4 Ricoeur, *Philosophy, Ethics, and Politics,* 12.

specialists. My greatest potential impact is there: the object is complex, but it is in a pedagogical space that I am intervening.

However, although this book has pedagogical goals, it is *not* a textbook. I am seeking to make an original contribution to a long-standing debate in the humanities about the tools we use to investigate the world, tools I would call *method* except that the term evokes a narrow category that I am trying to expand. This book finds its predecessors in a genre we might call "how to read" books (or "how to read books") that has flourished since the early twentieth century. These books include Mortimer Adler's *How to Read a Book* (published in 1940, with an updated edition co-authored by Charles van Dooren in 1972) and Harold Bloom's *How to Read and Why* (published in 2000).[5] They are frequently marked by what Karen Manarin describes as the "'reading crisis' trope,"[6] recognizable in the nostalgia for the putative lost art of reading, a reverence or veneration for an unjustly neglected canon, and a resistance to considerations (such as "'gender and sexuality' and 'multiculturalism'")[7] that some see as intrusive and exogenous to the field of literary studies. Not all examples of the genre employ this trope: Virginia Woolf's 1926 essay "How Should One Read a Book?" sees value in great writing but does not rehearse the narrative of decline, while, more recently, the contributors to Kaitlin Heller and Suzanne Conklin Akbari's *How We Read* provide a playful, open-ended engagement with the act of reading.[8] The question of how to read has even produced insightful Twitter threads.[9]

---

5 Mortimer J. Adler, *How to Read a Book: The Art of Getting a Liberal Education*; Mortimer J. Adler and Charles van Dooren, *How to Read a Book: The Classic Guide to Intelligent Reading*; Harold Bloom, *How to Read and Why*.

6 Karen Manarin, "Why Read?" 12.

7 Bloom, *How to Read and Why*, 23.

8 Virginia Woolf, "How Should One Read a Book?"; Kaitlin Heller and Suzanne Conklin Akbari, *How We Read: Tales, Fury, Nothing, Sound*.

9 Roy Pérez (Vanta Griege @ultramaricon), "These are tips I wrote for my students my students on how to read theory in a humanities/interdisciplinary context" (thread), Twitter, September 21, 2020, https://twitter.com/ultramaricon/status/1308099756510466049.

I share these writers' admiration of the classics, but not (in the case of Adler, van Dooren, and Bloom) their dismissal of the popular. I do not agree that "we can only learn from our 'betters,'"[10] perhaps because I am unsure who these "betters" are: Sappho and Homer can instruct us, but so can *Star Trek: Voyager*. Still, Adler has a passage in the 1940 edition of his book that is worth citing at length because he and I are, so to speak, on the very same page:

> There is only one situation that I can think of in which men and women make an effort to read better than they usually do. When they are in love and are reading a love letter, they read for all they are worth. They read every word three ways; they read between the lines and in the margins; they read the whole in terms of the parts, and each part in terms of the whole; they grow sensitive to context and ambiguity, to insinuation and implication; they perceive the color of words, the odor of phrases, and the weight of sentences.[11]

We should read, I argue, like we are in love.

My interest lies in discovering what the interpretation of metaphor, the figure of speech that links two dissimilar things, reveals about reading. I also consider texts, meaningful actions, and in the end, other people, all of which are like metaphors but on ever larger scales. In this respect, metaphor plays a paradoxical role: it is an object I examine but, through the comparisons I constantly make with it, it is also a tool I use to examine other objects. Metaphor, in its structure and logic, becomes a metaphor for texts, actions, and people.

Here is where the effects of my strategy of addressing this book to my students become clear. As I argue, a metaphor's meaning emerges in the space between its literal and figurative meanings. It is dynamic, rather than something we can pin down once and for all. I have sought therefore to leave that space open, which, more concretely, has meant employing a mode of argumentation that relies

---

10 Adler and van Dooren, *How to Read a Book*, 10.

11 Adler, *How to Read a Book*, 14.

as much on induction as it does on deduction. I have also included a wide range of images for this reason. Although some are diagrams I created to represent my argument visually, others I have repurposed from public domain sources, largely OldBookIllustrations.com, an archive of lovely pictures scanned from books published in the eighteenth, nineteenth, and early twentieth centuries.[12] To interpret these images, I ask the reader to find the link between them and the text, which is more abstract in some places than others. To explore the link between dissimilar objects—words and pictures—is to explore the space opened by metaphor. That process becomes another way to make sense of my argument.

That approach is the reading strategy I want to encourage. This book is about how texts, especially difficult ones, open a world. The point is not so much to comprehend these worlds as it is to discover and explore them.

---

12 I love online comics, and my choice of these images is intended, in a small way, as an homage to David Malki !'s *Wondermark* series (http://wondermark.com), in which Malki ! uses similarly old-fashioned images, likewise adding dialogue in cartoon bubbles.

Acknowledgements

———•———

Thank you to my many conversation partners in this project: Erin Burns, for her approach to the everyday practice of hermeneutics; Sam Rocha, for his books on phenomenology and love; Brenda Macdougall, for her generous insight into Indigenous methodologies. Thank you especially to Maryame Ichiba and Zixuan Zhao, for their engagement with early versions of the manuscript and the many ideas on which it draws as part of our doctoral methods seminar in Fall 2020.

Thank you to Ms. Parris, my Grade 12 English teacher, for her encouragement when I got carried away writing about Homeric similes.

Thank you to the Internet Archive (archive.org), the Project Gutenberg (Gutenberg.org), and the University of Ottawa library, for the access they provided to the many e-books I needed while hunkered down in my basement during the first part of the COVID-19 pandemic. Through them, I could engage even more partners in conversation.

Thank you to my mother, for the gift of an e-reader even before I knew I needed it.

Thank you to everyone at Athabasca University Press, especially Pamela Holway, for their enthusiasm and support of the pedagogical project of which this book is the second instalment. Thank you to the anonymous reviewers for their careful engagement with my argument. Thank you also to Peter Midgley for his thoughtful copyediting.

Finally, thank you, always and forever, to Ellie, Ben, and Kristi.

Sonst stünde dieser Stein entstellt und kurz
unter der Schultern durchsichtigem Sturz
und flimmerte nicht so wie Raubtierfelle

und bräche nicht aus allen seinen Rändern
aus wie ein Stern: denn da ist keine Stelle,
die dich nicht sieht.

> —Rainer Maria Rilke, from "Archaïscher
> Torso Apollos," in *Der Neuen Gedichte*

Introduction

What Is Reading?

———•———

Scenario 1. Imagine I'm a professor and you're a student. On the first day of class, you come into the classroom, sit down, and wait for me to arrive. I walk in, announce which class this is (in case anyone's in the wrong room), and hand out the syllabus. We read it together: the title of the class, when and where we meet, my contact information and office hours, the class rationale, a list of books, a set of class policies, the assignment descriptions, and a week-by-week breakdown of the readings. I ask if there are any questions. You do not raise your hand. No one raises their hand because there are no questions. It's the first day, so we call it good. "I'll see you next week," I say. You gather up your books and your copy of the syllabus, toss them in your bag, and leave.

A week later, when you come to class again, you remember nothing from the syllabus.

Scenario 2. Imagine I'm a professor and you're a student. On the first day of class, you come into the classroom, sit down, and wait for me to arrive. I walk in, set down an odd wooden box I'm carrying under my arm, and climb up on top of it. It's a soapbox, about a foot tall. With no warning, no explanation about what I'm doing or why (or even what class we're in), I open Lawrence Ferlinghetti's *A Coney Island of the Mind* and start reading—no, *declaiming*—the poem "I

3

Am Waiting": "I am waiting for my case to come up!" I declare, "and I am waiting for a rebirth of wonder!"

Wonder, indeed, you think to yourself. What the hell?

I go on, channelling my inner Beat poet, listing all the things I am waiting for: the Second Coming, my number to be called, "linnets and planets to fall like rain." I start out slowly, then read faster, until I reach the climactic ending—my favourite part of the entire poem: "I am awaiting / perpetually and forever / a renaissance of wonder!"[1]

I step down from my soapbox. You do not clap. I pick up my box and leave. You sit, puzzled, not sure whether class is done, or whether it even started.

A week later, when you come to class again, you are still puzzling over the poem and the weird-ass professor who read it.

What do we make of these scenarios? They are the same in every way but two: what I read and how you react. The link between those two things—the first as cause, the second as effect—is the focus of this book. In Scenario 1, I transmit the content of the syllabus, but the interaction is so routine that you soon forget what I've said. Five weeks later, as the midterm approaches, you will send me an earnest email asking what's on it, and I will tell you to check the syllabus because we talked about the midterm on the first day of class. You will read the syllabus as if seeing it for the first time. In Scenario 2, I transmit no content, other than that of a poem, but poetic content is different from that of a syllabus. Still, you will not forget the experience. In fact, it was so strange you might just add a comment about it to my Rate My Professor page when the course is done. In contrast to Scenario 1, you remember something about the day.

Briankle Chang, from whose work on deconstruction and communication I've adapted my scenarios, writes that in situations such as I describe, "Communication can actually take place when it *appears*

---

1 Lawrence Ferlinghetti, "I Am Waiting." Ferlinghetti is too discreet to use so many exclamation points. They are a product of my enthusiastic reading.

not to take place, and it can appear to take place when it actually fails to even begin."[2] In Scenario 1, I appear to have communicated certain content, that of the syllabus, but because you forget it, I have communicated nothing. In contrast, in Scenario 2, I have transmitted no content at all, at least not in the same sense as in Scenario 1, and yet you have retained it. I have succeeded where I appeared to fail. The nature of that success and the dichotomy of these experiences is what I explore in this book.

To see how, let's consider two more scenarios.

Scenario 3. Imagine I'm a writer and you're a reader. You pick up my book, on the first page of which I have written: "This book is a humanist's answer to the question of method. In communication studies, 'method' describes the tools we use to study the world. This book is about those tools."

You appreciate the sentences' clarity (even if the mention of humanism seems a bit out of place—but you'll overlook your puzzlement for now). How lovely, you say to yourself as you set the book down, thinking perhaps that you might return to it later.

You do not return to it later. Something more interesting comes along, and the book sits forgotten on the shelf.

Scenario 4. Imagine I'm a writer and you're a reader. You pick up my book, on the first page of which I have written:

> *Scenario 1.* Imagine I'm a professor and you're a student. On the first day of class, you come into the classroom, sit down, and wait for me to arrive. I walk in, announce which class this is (in case anyone's in the wrong room), and hand out the syllabus.

You scan a little further, and you see there's a second scenario, one about a guerilla poetry reading, something about waiting for Beat poets. How weird, you say. What on earth is this book *about*?

---

2 Briankle G. Chang, "Deconstructing Communication," 254.

Of course, you see what I'm doing here. I want you to remember this book—I want you to read more of it, so my cold open is meant to knock you off balance. I want to make you feel disoriented because you'll remember the feeling far more than you'll remember some platitude about method in communication studies. This *is* a book about method, and I *am* a humanist talking about the tools we use to pry open the world to expose its inner workings. By dropping you into the middle of my thoughts, but then giving you some sort of structure to lean on, I hope you will remember the content of my argument, too. The shock of confusion, followed by stability when you find your footing: that is the way communication succeeds. It's about the relation between Scenarios 1 and 2, or 3 and 4.

This relation takes the structure of a metaphor. You probably learned in elementary school that a metaphor is a comparison you make without the words *like* or *as* (which would be a simile). "The sun is a lion," you learned to say. Your teachers weren't wrong, although metaphor is more interesting, and knottier, than that. (For one thing, a simile is a type of metaphor, your teacher's lessons notwithstanding. More on that below.) As rhetoric scholar Kenneth Burke describes it, metaphor is "a device for seeing something *in terms of* something else. It brings out the thisness of a that, or the thatness of a this."[3] In the *Iliad* and the *Odyssey*, for instance, Homer often describes the sea as "wine-dark." The metaphor—comparing wine and sea—has long puzzled scholars. Was the sea really deep red, they ask?[4] Graham Harman, a philosopher of art, uses the image to talk about how metaphor works: "The Homeric sea, when described as 'wine-dark,' is so out of joint with wine that it is no longer the sensual sea of everyday experience and literal language. The sea is now withdrawn and mysterious, orbited by sensuous wine-qualities."[5]

---

3 Kenneth Burke, "Four Master Tropes," 421–22.

4 See John Noble Wilford, "Homer's Sea: Wine Dark?"

5 Graham Harman, *Art and Objects*, 68. For example, in Book 5 of the *Odyssey*, the nymph Calypso is lamenting that she cannot stop Odysseus from returning home, despite promising him immortality: "O ye gods, that a mortal man should abide

Metaphor tells us something literal (the sea is dark like wine) and, at the very same time, something more than literal. That is what I mean when I say "the structure of a metaphor": it's a literal meaning (one that might make little sense, as in Homer's case) that points to something mysterious outside itself.

In this respect, what if I said that in Scenario 2, I intended "I Am Waiting" to serve as a metaphor for the syllabus? You might respond with confusion. That's okay. It means you understand my argument, even if you feel confused. The confusion, if I've done this right, should push you to look for meaning beyond the surface of what I am saying (and what Ferlinghetti is saying). You're trying to decipher what I've said. Think of your confusion not as something blocking you but as something pushing you to ask, what can this claim—that "I Am Waiting" is a syllabus—possibly *mean*? The answer to that question—that's the mystery you're looking to explore.

The truth is, I was lying when I said that "I Am Waiting" lacked syllabus-like content. On the surface, it's a poem about waiting and about wonder. Ferlinghetti is waiting for a lot of things, but all of them point to the experience of opening oneself up to the world. I read "I Am Waiting" because it provokes a sense of *thaumazein*, or the astonishment, according to Aristotle, from which philosophy springs. If I tell you "I want you to recapture the wonder for the world you had as a child," you'll stare at me with the jaded expression you have learned to adopt when anyone repeats platitudes about the feelings you had (or didn't have) as a kid. You'll forget the platitudes, like you forget the content of a syllabus. That communication will fail.

If I surprise you, on the other hand, so that in your confusion, you come to wonder what I'm doing, then you might hold onto the

---

with me. Him I saved when he was bestriding the keel and all alone, for Zeus had smitten his swift ship with his bright thunder-bolt, and had shattered it in the midst of the wine-dark sea." Homer, *The Odyssey*, 179.

wonder longer, and what you discover in pursuing it is something you'll own.

That's the purpose of this book.

Catalyst Books

If I wrote, "This book is about how to read difficult texts," it would be true but prosaic. My first readers are graduate students in a seminar about communication method at the University of Ottawa, where I teach, and together we will read difficult texts. It's a learned skill, one I will use this book to help them acquire.

It would be better if I wrote, "This book is about how to read *like you mean it*." It's about looking for something you feel you have lost, like the woman in the biblical parable looking for her lost coin,[6] or my students looking for their lost phones. The woman and my students dig through the room, picking up cushions to look underneath, sweeping the floor, asking each time, *Is it here?* This book is about reading with that same appetite to find something. We'll develop the questions to ask as we go.

The ideas come out of my own experience as a student, when two types of books influenced me profoundly. One kind was impenetrable, presenting a wall of dense text that made me feel angry and confused. Mikhail Bakhtin's *The Dialogic Imagination*, and in particular the chapter "Discourse in the Novel," is the first I remember in this category. I read it as an undergraduate in my third year, and I made it to the end out of spite. I also came back to it years later, drawn by the visceral response it had provoked in me in the first place. If I felt angry and confused, it was because I sensed something compelling within the text but beyond my grasp. What mattered was the force of the emotion, not its negative tenor, and I felt driven to discover what it was I sensed. Since then, Bakhtin's ideas of dialogue, rooted in

---

6 Luke 15:8–10.

the material circumstances where talking takes place, have shaped the course of my thinking.

The second type of book was a catalyst. These books were intermediary texts, not in their difficulty (they were not necessarily easier or harder than the impenetrable texts that were a thorn in my shoe) but in the role they played: I could grasp them, and they gave me the conceptual tools I needed to make sense of the impenetrable texts. The authors showed their work, the way my math teachers in elementary school made me show my work. Karl Marx and Friedrich Engels's *The German Ideology* was one such text, through which I came to read Bakhtin and those in his circle, such as V. N. Vološinov, whose *Marxism and the Philosophy of Language* now pervades my thinking. The impenetrable books would have remained enigmas were it not for the catalyst books.

Here I am writing a catalyst book. In a broad sense, it's about the mechanics of scholarly work—the tools we use to generate insight into our world and the lives we lead, to make claims, and to support them. In a narrow sense, it develops an idea I mentioned at the end of an earlier book, *The Art of Communication in a Polarized World*. That book opens with the question, "How can we change another person's mind?" It proposes an eclectic set of tools drawn from classical rhetoric, *Star Wars*, performance art, and George Orwell's *Nineteen Eighty-Four* (among other things), that allow us to make arguments to put people in a position to see the world in a new way. It ends by doubling back to the beginning. "How do we change people's minds?" it asks. "By opening ourselves to the possibility that they might change our minds, too."[7] *The Art of Communication* was about speaking, but the conclusion I reached was about listening. In this book, I speak of reading, but the idea is the same: it's about how we open ourselves to others and to ideas that scare us because we don't understand them.

---

7 Kyle Conway, *The Art of Communication in a Polarized World*, 128.

In this respect, talking about scholarly method is really an excuse to talk about something bigger. The field of communication has plenty of method textbooks. This isn't one of them.

Method in the Social Sciences

If I were to describe method, I would say it is "the word we use to describe how researchers find and use data to understand and explain a phenomenon, in ways frequently influenced by their chosen theoretical paradigm."[8] We study method to acquire a set of tools. We talk about the uses to which we put them and the ways they help us persuade others that our explanation of a phenomenon is correct, or at least better than the ones that preceded it.

When I teach methods, I like to use Gerianne Merrigan, Carole Huston, and Russell Johnston's textbook *Communication Research Methods* because Merrigan and her co-authors take a reflexive approach, embracing epistemological questions about how we know what we know (or think we know). To explore the tools of inquiry, they develop a model for building an argument—the *claim-evidence-warrant* model—initially proposed by Stephen Toulmin.[9] The relationship between each of the terms guides researchers as they collect and use evidence: a claim is the "central assertion" on which an argument is built; evidence is the "grounds that support a claim"; and a warrant is the "the primary means of linking research

---

8 This definition derives largely from *Communication Research Methods*, by Gerianne Merrigan, Carole L. Huston, and Russell Johnston, but the paraphrase is my own.

9 Stephen Toulmin, *Human Understanding: The Collective Use and Evolution of Concepts*, and Stephen Toulmin, Richard Rieke, and Allan Janik, *An Introduction to Reasoning*. Note that Merrigan and her co-authors speak of "data" instead of "evidence." I'm avoiding the word "data" because I've observed that for my students, it tends to evoke ideas of numbers and measurement, whereas I, like the authors of *Communication Research Methods*, want to talk about a wider range of modes of observation.

claims to data or evidence" or the "standard the researcher applies to assess the merits of the data supporting a claim."[10]

They describe three different paradigms researchers follow as they put this model to use. The discovery paradigm presumes that knowledge is something to acquire through observation; the interpretive paradigm, that it's something to be contextualized and made sense of; and the critical paradigm, that it serves as the basis of social critique.[11] To be sure, my description of these paradigms is schematic. Researchers often work between paradigms, the insights of one shaping work people do in another. Their value here is heuristic: identifying them brings the assumptions scholars make about the nature of reality and the purpose of describing it into clear relief. For instance, the discovery paradigm approaches reality as singular and knowable through observation and measurement. The purpose of research is to represent it accurately. This paradigm is common among behavioural psychologists, quantitative sociologists, and others who aspire to standards of rigour as understood by the "hard" (that is, positivist or empiricist) sciences. Students in my classes often treat it as the default mode against which others must be measured, finding the others lacking in comparison.

What's important about the other paradigms, however, is that they conceptualize the world—and rigour—differently. The tools they provide answer a different set of questions, which the discovery paradigm cannot answer. The interpretive paradigm, used by people in anthropology, sociology, and various branches of communication studies, is more concerned with *symbolic* worlds and thus treats reality as multiple and socially constructed. Within it, the goal of research is to explain how people make sense of their lives. The critical paradigm, used in critical and cultural studies, also deals with socially constructed symbolic worlds, but it adds a concern about social inequality. The purpose of research is to bring about social change.

---

10 Merrigan, Huston, and Johnston, *Communication Research Methods*, 8.

11 Merrigan, Huston, and Johnston, *Communication Research Methods*, 36.

Each of these paradigms comes with its own set of values and, consequently, the goals researchers have when they make claims and the nature of the warrants that support them (table 1).[12] The discovery paradigm places value on the related qualities of precision and predictability. Researchers work to be as accurate as possible in ways that allow them to make predictions about similar phenomena, demonstrating cause-and-effect relationships. The warrant for their claims—the grounds on which other scholars evaluate them—are thus reliability (are observations consistent "over time, across, settings, subjects, and instruments"?) and validity (are they applicable "to other settings, persons, or situations"?).[13] In contrast, the interpretive paradigm values rich description, which scholars use to make sense of complex symbolic systems. The warrants for their claims relate to plausibility (do they make more sense than alternative explanations?) and the credibility of the researcher (are they in a position to know what they claim to know?). The critical paradigm is similar to the interpretive paradigm: it seeks to untangle the social and political contradictions that characterize a society and explain how people's actions perpetuate them. Scholars evaluate these claims based on their coherence (do they explain contradictions across different facets of a community's social life?) and researchers' reflexivity about the position they occupy (do they take into account how their position shapes their interpretations?).

Method in the humanities takes a different form, although people use a range of tools in overlapping, complementary ways, much as in the social sciences.[14] One distinguishing feature for my purposes

---

12 This section derives from Merrigan, Huston, and Johnston, *Communication Research Methods*, chap. 6.

13 Merrigan, Huston, and Johnston, *Communication Research Methods*, 298 and 301. For another useful iteration of this analysis, see Egon G. Guba and Yvonna S. Lincoln, "Competing Paradigms in Qualitative Research."

14 Terry Eagleton gives a good sense of the range of methods in literary studies, for instance, in *Literary Theory: An Introduction*. Although his focus is theory, in the humanities, modes of inquiry often grow out of the theoretical frameworks scholars

Table 1. The values, goals, and warrants of the discovery, interpretive, and critical paradigms

	Discovery paradigm	Interpretive paradigm	Critical paradigm
Values	Precision and predictability	Rich description	Social and political action, justice
Goal of claim / evidence	Demonstrate causality	Make sense of complex symbolic systems	Explain social, political contradictions
Warrant	Reliability and validity of explanation	Plausibility of explanation, researcher credibility	Coherence of explanation, researcher reflexivity / positionality

Source: Adapted from Merrigan, Huston, and Johnston, *Communication Research Methods*, 100.

in this book is the way humanistic method inverts the relationship between the object of study and the world to which it belongs. In contrast to conventional social scientific method, which provides tools to learn about the object one is studying, humanistic method provides tools to use the object of study—the texts we read, in the broadest possible sense—to understand something more about the world. As we'll see, this inversion changes the nature of the values, claims, evidence, and warrants we can use to build an argument. As we'll also see, it provides a means to rethink conventional social scientific method.

How do we understand humanistic method? We turn to the idea of metaphor.

---

employ. What I learned about method as a literature major at the University of North Dakota came largely from applying the ideas in Eagleton's book.

Metaphor: Two Models

"Metaphor is not only one of the most commonly used figures of speech in everyday language," observes Annemie Halsema, but "it also has attracted more philosophical interest than any other figure of speech."[15] It's popular because of its fundamentally creative structure, bringing together things that are not alike and forcing us to find the links between them.

Philosophers have been asking how metaphors work at least since Aristotle, who provides two models for understanding them. The first treats metaphor as a form of *substitution*, where one object replaces another with shared traits. The second treats metaphor as an invitation to explore the dynamic relationship of resemblance between two objects. These models find support in Aristotle's treatises on rhetoric (the art of speech-making) and poetics (the art of poetry and tragedy). In the *Poetics*, he identifies four types of metaphor: it is "the application of an alien name by transference either from genus to species, or from species to genus, or from species to species, or by analogy, that is, proportion."[16] In the *Rhetoric*, he explains what makes it persuasive: "Now strange words simply puzzle us; ordinary words convey only what we know already; it is from metaphor that we can best get hold of something fresh."[17] Metaphor works through surprise: by substituting an elegant or more noble word for a plain word, it pleases the listener, who comes to see the object in a new way. The sea is no longer merely the sea, in Homer's world, but now deeper and darker like wine.

One of the commonest ways to interpret these definitions is to see metaphor as a type of riddle. Aristotle, for example, says, "Good riddles do, in general, provide us with satisfactory metaphors: for metaphors imply riddles, and therefore a good riddle can furnish

---

15 Annemie Halsema, "Metaphor," 79.

16 Aristotle, *Poetics*, Section 3, Part 21, 1457b.

17 Aristotle, *Rhetoric*, Book 3, Part 10, 1410b.

a good metaphor."[18] Listeners figure out how an object is part of a broad category (or, to adopt Aristotle's language, how a species belongs to a genus), or how a category stands in for a specific object, or how one object is like another, or, perhaps the most complex task, they work out an analogy in the form "A is to B as X is to Y." (What term completes the sentence, "The sea is to _____ as wine is to the colour red"? Or is colour even the right category for comparison? Perhaps mystery or emotion would be better.)

It's the puzzle that engages listeners and, through that engagement, persuades them. It is also the idea that grounds the substitution model: to solve the riddle—to explain the metaphor—is to find the common trait. Consider a famous riddle from Lewis Carroll's *Alice's Adventures in Wonderland* (figure 1). Alice has followed a fretful rabbit down a hole into a world that follows neither logic nor the laws of physics. As she wanders about, she happens upon an odd party, attended by a Mad Hatter, a March Hare, and a Dormouse. She sits at their table, and when the Hatter obliquely suggests she should cut her hair, she scolds him for being rude. The Hatter replies with a non sequitur: "Why is a raven like a writing-desk?" Alice responds:

> "I'm glad they've begun asking riddles.—I believe I can guess that," she added aloud.
>
> "Do you mean that you think you can find out the answer to it?" said the March Hare.
>
> "Exactly so," said Alice.
>
> "Then you should say what you mean," the March Hare went on.
>
> "I do," Alice hastily replied; "at least—at least I mean what I say—that's the same thing, you know."
>
> "Not the same thing a bit!" said the Hatter. "You might just as well say that 'I see what I eat' is the same thing as 'I eat what I see'!"

---

18 Aristotle, *Rhetoric*, Book 3, Part 2, 1405b. Aristotle expands on this idea of metaphor as riddle in Book 3, Part 11.

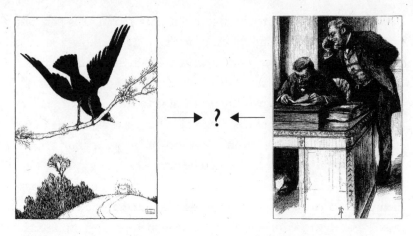

Figure 1. How is a raven like a writing desk? What trait connects them? Sources: Modified from William Heath Robinson, *Flapped Black Wings* (1917) and Amédée Forestier, *Unintelligible Writing* (1890). OldBookIllustrations.com.

"You might just as well say," added the March Hare, "that 'I like what I get' is the same thing as 'I get what I like'!"

"You might just as well say," added the Dormouse, who seemed to be talking in his sleep, "that 'I breathe when I sleep' is the same thing as 'I sleep when I breathe'!"

"It *is* the same thing with you," said the Hatter, and here the conversation dropped, and the party sat silent for a minute, while Alice thought over all she could remember about ravens and writing-desks, which wasn't much.[19]

It's a rich passage. We can solve the riddle—and the metaphor—if only we can find the thing ravens and writing desks share in common. The Hatter is no help: when Alice gives up and asks him, he says, "I haven't the slightest idea."[20] Carroll, tired of being pestered for a response, eventually said, "Because it can produce a few notes, tho they are very flat; and it is never put with the wrong end in front!"

---

19 Lewis Carroll, *Alice's Adventures in Wonderland*, 83–84.

20 Carroll, *Alice's Adventures in Wonderland*, 86.

Author Aldous Huxley proposed enigmatically, "Because there is a 'b' in both and an 'n' in neither," while Samuel Lloyd, a famous puzzle-maker from the late nineteenth century, said simply, "Poe wrote on both."[21]

What is the Hatter's comment that "I see what I eat" is the same as "I eat what I see" if not a fortuitous comment on metaphor? "Wait!" you object. "Let's back up a second. 'Why is a raven like a writing-desk?' That's a simile—it has the word *like*!" You're right, of course. But its function is the same, as Aristotle writes: "The simile . . . is a metaphor, differing from it only in the way it is put; and just because it is longer it is less attractive."[22] Metaphor's defining quality, which simile shares, is the way it moves ideas "from one realm to another, non-intersecting realm."[23]

But the Hatter's riddle also shows the shortcomings of the substitution model because the answer appears to exhaust the question. Once you know it, what else is there to do but move on? Indeed, according to the philosopher Paul Ricoeur, the idea that a metaphor is no more than a puzzle was a symptom of the intellectual myopia that led to rhetoric's historical decline as a discipline. By the middle of the twentieth century, the study of rhetoric consisted largely in the cataloguing of different tropes or figures of speech. The problem was that if metaphor is just a neat trick, that is, "if an exhaustive paraphrase of the metaphor . . . can be given, then the metaphor says nothing new . . . teaching us nothing."[24]

---

21 These answers all come from Esther Inglis-Arkell, "The Answer to the Most Famous Unanswerable Fantasy Riddle." According to Inglis-Arkell, Carroll spelled *never* as *nevar*, or *raven* backwards, a pun that was lost when a fastidious proof-reader corrected it.

22 Aristotle, *Rhetoric*, Book 3, Part 10, 1410b. Aristotle's assertion is not entirely uncontroversial, however. Everything hinges on the relationship implied by the word *like* or by the verb *to be*. See Paul Ricoeur, *The Rule of Metaphor: The Creation of Meaning in Language*, 291–302.

23 Ricoeur, *Rule of Metaphor*, 280.

24 Ricoeur, *Rule of Metaphor*, 52. Ricoeur's history of rhetoric's decline is specific to the French system of education. In the United States, for instance, it played a

But if we look deeper, metaphor hides a paradox, which is key to understanding the second model, which we can call the *tension* model. Although metaphor is about similarity—about finding a common trait—it is *also* about elevated speech, if we follow Aristotle. The thing to which the object is compared is *more* than the object itself. If it weren't, there'd be no point in the metaphor—the object would be sufficient on its own. Because the first object cannot be assimilated into the second, metaphor produces difference in similarity.

In effect, metaphor says two contradictory things at once: the sea is like wine, and—because wine is darker and more mysterious than the sea—it is not like wine at all. In other words, at a literal level, metaphors are nonsensical: except for being wet, the sea is *nothing* like wine. It's salty, you can't drink it, and its hue is more blue-green than burgundy. Homer's assertion is so strange, in fact, that scholars have asked, were the Greeks simply colour-blind? Did they not have a word for "blue"? Did they put some sort of dye in their wine to change its colour?[25]

Ricoeur calls this facet of metaphor—the falseness of its literal meaning—the "literal *is not*."[26] Yet, in spite of this inherent falseness, it is clear that the comparison evokes something powerful. If it didn't, Homer's readers would not still be trying to discern its meaning three millennia later. But this second facet—its figurative truth, which Ricoeur calls the "metaphorical *is*"—is tough to pin down.[27] We are pulled in opposite directions between different levels of meaning: the words in front of us have, on the one hand, a literal meaning that is accessible but not true, and on the other hand, a metaphorical meaning that is true but not easily accessible.

different role, as many universities had speech departments that later transformed into communication departments.

25 Wilford, "Homer's Sea."

26 Ricoeur, *Rule of Metaphor*, 253.

27 Ricoeur, *Rule of Metaphor*, 253.

What do we do with this contradiction? To quote Ricoeur's philosophically dense language, "There is no other way to do justice to the notion of metaphorical truth than to include the critical incision of the (literal) 'is not' within the ontological vehemence of the (metaphorical) 'is.'"[28] By the "ontological vehemence of the (metaphorical) 'is,'" Ricoeur means the impulse to embrace figurative meaning in ways that cause us to abandon the far more frustrating literal meaning—the "literal *is not*." This is something we cannot do. Despite its frustrations, we cannot wish away a literal meaning that, even if it is false, is still present. We must account for it, even if—*especially* if—it contradicts a metaphor's figurative meaning. Here is where the "literal *is not*" makes its "critical incision."

But before we delve into these questions, let's take a step back. Is your head spinning? These abstractions can be impenetrable, especially if you're encountering them (as will be the case for many of my students) for the first time. In fact, I'm counting on it. The first step in reading hard texts is to embrace the disorienting effect they have on us. This act runs counter to our compulsive need, learned over years of school, to be right, or at least not to be wrong. Formal education, with its emphasis on extrinsic factors such as grades, presents us with a false choice between mastery and failure.

Truth be told, the terms *mastery* and *failure* are misleading. *Mastery* seems to imply that a person has full command of a concept or collection of ideas, when in fact, writers (and professors) have just learned to project an emotional detachment from the subject matter that they use to convince readers (and students) that they know what they're talking about. I discovered this fact only when I became a writer and a professor. As a student, I was persuaded that writers knew what they were talking about, but what I saw was their finished document, which showed no signs of the self-doubt they worked through to create it. As a writer, I know those moments of self-doubt well. The thing readers and students must realize, in Rita

---

28 Ricoeur, *Rule of Metaphor*, 302.

Felski's words, is that "Critical detachment, in this light, is not an absence of mood but one manifestation of it—a certain orientation toward one's subject, a way of making one's argument matter. It is tied to the cultivation of an intellectual persona that is highly prized in literary studies and beyond: suspicious, knowing, self-conscious, hardheaded, tirelessly vigilant."[29]

Failure is misleading because it seems to imply a finality or point of no return, when in fact what learning really requires is struggle and practice. North American universities (the ones I know best) do us no favours here. As I put together my syllabi, for instance, I must identify learning objectives, which are an unfortunate symptom of the trend to treat education as a means to an end. That instrumentalization works against what I want to accomplish as a teacher. The problem, as Hannah Arendt wrote half a century ago, is that that utility, or the use to which we put something, has come to replace meaningfulness, or the intrinsic value it has for us, and that "utility established as meaning generates meaninglessness."[30] In other words, the ends to which we use something are not ends at all. Instead they become a means to something else. Students might read a book to acquire new ideas, but those new ideas become means to write a paper, which becomes a means to earn a degree, which becomes a means to finding a job, and so on. If students resent having to read something for class, who can blame them? We treat education like an elaborate quiz show, when really, reading like you mean it is more like learning a craft and cultivating your talent.

We'll spend the rest of the book parsing metaphor's paradoxical *is not/is* structure. What we'll discover is that, ultimately, this structure is liberating: "Metaphor is living by virtue of the fact that it introduces the spark of imagination into a 'thinking more' at the conceptual

---

29 Rita Felski, *The Limits of Critique*, 6.

30 Hannah Arendt, *The Human Condition*, 154.

level. This struggle to 'think more,' guided by the 'vivifying principle,' is the 'soul' of interpretation."[31]

Method Through the Lens of Metaphor

Let's return to the question of method. We can look at metaphor, for instance, through the concerns explored above. What does a metaphor-centric humanistic method presuppose about the nature of reality? What values does it privilege? What goals are served by its claims, and what warrants support them? We can also observe social scientific method through the lens of metaphor. What questions does metaphor raise for the critical, interpretive, and discovery paradigms? Must we re-evaluate the conclusions arrived at within those paradigms? If so, how?

In answer to the first questions, this mode of humanistic inquiry treats reality as knowable, but not directly: it is observable in the tension between objects and the things to which we compare them; or, framed differently, between the literal and figurative levels of meaning. This is what John Durham Peters means when he says we must let the texts we read "instruct us, by their distance and familiarity."[32] This mode of inquiry values reflexive, creative expression. Both traits are important: we are reflexive when we navigate between the different levels of meaning, taking into account how and where we move. We are creative when we arrive someplace new, one result being that humanistic work is frequently speculative, rather than falsifiable (that is, having the capacity to be proven right or wrong), as in the discovery paradigm.[33] The warrant for speculative arguments is persuasiveness: does the explanation we offer account for the complexities we identify in the object of study? Sarah Maitland, building

---

31 Ricoeur, *Rule of Metaphor*, 358.

32 John Durham Peters, *Speaking into the Air: A History of the Idea of Communication*, 36.

33 See Jonathan Culler, *Literary Theory: A Very Short Introduction*, especially 14–15.

on Ricoeur, turns to a legal example (a legal *metaphor*!) to explain how scholars make their case:

> In order to ensure that a judge's ruling is not arbitrary, their interpretation is subjected to validation—precedents are consulted, evidence is presented, arguments are made, interpretations are defended or prosecuted, and, on the balance of probability and in the light of the available evidence, conclusions are weighed. Like the parties to a legal case, readers must build their case for support, attempting to prove beyond all reasonable doubt that their interpretation is the most probable in the light of all that is known about a text [again, broadly speaking]. We submit our understanding to the scrutiny of the court of public opinion, we advance an argument and we await a ruling.[34]

In chapter 4 of this book, I will subject my argument to exactly these criteria.

Where do other paradigms employ metaphor? Its use is easiest to discern in the critical and interpretive paradigms because they focus on questions of meaning. Within the critical paradigm, metaphors help illustrate the competing interpretations of the world that perpetuate inequalities scholars seek to address. Similarly, within the interpretive paradigm, making sense of complex symbolic systems means engaging reflexively with competing explanations.

In the discovery paradigm, we must look harder. Whenever we ascribe meaning to human behaviour, we are interpreting it, and it's in that interpretation that we find metaphor. In art, for example, we might contend that "a certain picture that *possesses* the colour grey *expresses* sadness."[35] We're explaining one aspect of the picture—its colour—in unrelated terms—its emotional register. Similarly, in discovery-oriented research, we might contend that an action expresses a mental state, when all we can observe directly is the action itself. Whenever social scientists develop models that

34 Sarah Maitland, *What Is Cultural Translation?* 133–34.
35 Ricoeur, *Rule of Metaphor*, 276.

explain behaviour in terms of something else, the structure of their comparison is metaphorical to the degree that ideas move from one realm to another.

Consider one of the most influential social scientific articles about interpersonal communication, Charles Berger and Richard Calabrese's "Some Explorations in Initial Interaction and Beyond: Toward a Developmental Theory of Interpersonal Communication," which describes how people interact when they first meet. Berger and Calabrese argue that as strangers become more comfortable with each other, their behaviour changes. The more they speak, for example, the less they feel uncertain, which in turn causes them to speak more. Observations such as these lead them to propose seven axioms from which they derive twenty-one testable theorems.

The article represents one of the "major examples of communication theories based on formal logic,"[36] yet it is grounded in metaphorical explanations. Berger and Calabrese's third axiom provides a useful illustration: "High levels of uncertainty cause increases in information seeking behavior. As uncertainty levels decline, information seeking behavior decreases."[37] In simpler terms, people who have just met ask each other a lot of questions, an action that, according to Berger and Calabrese, indicates their uncertainty about each other. As they grow more familiar, they make more statements (figure 2).

In effect, Berger and Calabrese ask what it means to pose questions quickly or slowly. But their answer—that these different rates indicate levels of certainty—is not directly observable: all that they can measure (measurement reflecting the values and warrant of the discovery paradigm) is the rate at which people ask questions. The interpretation requires a leap from one realm (that of observation) to another, non-intersecting realm (that of meaning). This is to

---

36 Merrigan, Huston, and Johnston, *Communication Research Methods*, 5.

37 Charles R. Berger and Richard J. Calabrese, "Some Explorations in Initial Interaction and Beyond: Toward a Developmental Theory of Interpersonal Communication," 103.

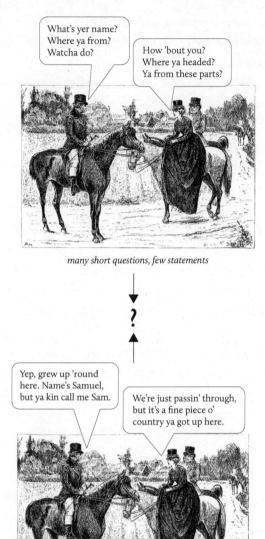

many short questions, few statements

few short questions, more statements

Figure 2. Certainty as a term linking different rates at which strangers ask each other questions or make statements. Source: Modified from George Du Maurier, *One or Two Questions* (1866). OldBookIllustrations.com.

say, their conclusion requires a passage through metaphor. As a result, we must be attentive to the paradox described in previous sections. Practically speaking, we must recognize that there are other possible explanations for their observations, for instance in cultural contexts where rates of question-asking might not indicate levels of certainty.

What, then, is the relationship between social scientific and humanistic methods? Where their concerns intersect, they serve as a check on each other. The paradox of metaphor draws Berger and Calabrese's conclusions into question, for instance, but it does not negate them. They remain sound within the bounds established by their respective warrants. They could even serve as support for claims a humanist might make in Maitland's court of public opinion. Arguments can be made more persuasive (persuasiveness being the warrant for humanistic method) by amassing more evidence, although whether it comes from discovery-oriented research or humanistic inquiry, that evidence, too, is subject to the paradox of metaphor.

Peering at the social sciences through the lens of metaphor ultimately reveals the degree to which the meaning we make of the world, regardless of our conceptual paradigm, is provisional. Humanistic method complements social scientific method, even as metaphor, which is central to the humanities, pulls back against it.

Chapter Overview: Getting Lost, Finding Our Way Back

Early in my teaching career, I was asked to present ideas about how to be successful to incoming first-year students. I gave them a simple formula: *Allow yourself to get lost. Then find your way back.* Not only are feelings of confusion normal, I told them, but they're also the key to learning. If we memorize things, it might seem like we've learned them, but we lose them quickly. If, on the other hand, they frustrate us, we can make them ours. (If a professor reads the syllabus on the first day of class, students will forget it. But if a professor reads a poem . . .)

In the chapters that follow, I describe how we harness that confusion. Metaphor plays multiple roles. First, in the distinction between the "literal *is not*" and the "metaphorical *is*," it provides a strategy for reading difficult texts. Confusion, I argue, is a reasonable response when we read things that cannot be true, as is the case for metaphor's literal meaning. We must look for meaning elsewhere, at the figurative level, and in so doing, develop interpretations supported by persuasive arguments.

Each of the following chapters describes a step in that process by exploring different metaphors for reading. Chapters 1 and 2 focus on the "literal *is not*." Chapter 1 proposes that *to read is to feel lost*. In the past three decades, there has been a running argument about the qualities of good academic writing, the implication being that the worst books in the humanities and social sciences amount to nothing more than nonsensical incantations of magic words meant to intimidate readers or make their authors look smart. This chapter explores those debates and the anxiety behind them to argue that, contrary to what critics contend, the confusion caused by difficult writing is valuable for the way it releases readers to explore metaphorical meaning. Chapter 2 proposes that *to read is to wander*. Being released to explore is one thing; doing so productively is another. This chapter asks what stories like that of the Israelites wandering in the wilderness (read as allegory) can tell us about wandering in search of meaning in a difficult text.

Chapters 3 and 4 focus on the "metaphorical *is*." Chapter 3 proposes that *to read is to feel love*. When, through wandering, we find an anchor or perspective, we experience a feeling of euphoria that is the inverse of the fear from chapter 1. The Greeks identified this feeling as eros, which this chapter, following Plato in the *Phaedrus* and Sappho in her poem known as Fragment 31, explores as a drive we feel pushing us toward the object of investigation. Chapter 4 proposes that *to read is to be free*. We cannot give ourselves over to the euphoria of metaphor in an unrestrained way because we would lose connection with literal meaning. Here we see that the confusion created by literal meaning remains valuable. Freedom is the inverse of wandering: it is living within the *is* of metaphor and the bounds imposed by the *is not* of literal sense. Less cryptically, it is the ability to make sense of—to interpret—difficult texts, not by inventing meaning from whole cloth, but by pulling against the literal meaning to which we remain nonetheless bound. Freedom in this sense is not absolute, but rather a function of greater movement, an idea I demonstrate by using social scientific studies of reading to evaluate my metaphorical claims.

Throughout these chapters, we explore a paradox: sometimes, what appears as communication is non-communication, such as in my example about syllabus reading. When we try to pin a text down, its meaning escapes us. Our reach exceeds our grasp. Instead, what we must do is let go of our desire to know a text as an object. In relinquishing control, we come unexpectedly to appropriate its meaning—to make it our own. Non-communication becomes communication.

The conclusion returns to the question that prompted this book: how do we listen meaningfully to others? How do we open ourselves to the possibility that others might change our minds? To answer these questions, I propose one more metaphor: *to read is to live with other people*. What we learn from the discussion about fear, wandering, love, and freedom is that to live with others, we must recognize that the tensions between the overlapping symbolic worlds we all inhabit are no more resolvable than the tensions between the literal and metaphorical levels of meaning. I insist, however, that we're getting a bargain: in exchange for a certainty that was never ours in the first place, we get new worlds to explore. We get to negotiate meaning in an ongoing way, a situation Ricoeur describes as that of "linguistic hospitality . . . where the pleasure of dwelling in the other's language is balanced by the pleasure of receiving the foreign word at home, in one's own welcoming house."[38]

---

38 Paul Ricoeur, *On Translation*, 10.

1

To Read Is to Feel Lost

Do you know the weirdest thing about writing?[1] Readers. I imagine my readers as I write, but I really don't know a lot about them. For this book, for instance, my first readers are my students. I'm putting together slides for lectures for a graduate seminar I will teach next semester about communication method. As I write, I imagine myself giving my lectures: we're in a room, I project the slides on a screen, and whenever I make a point that's obscure or convoluted, my students stop me and ask what I mean.

But that doesn't mean that *you* are one of my students (and even if you are, we're not sitting in a room together right now, as I write). If you're reading this book, then I must have succeeded in publishing it, and you, sitting in Reykjavík or Buenos Aires or Chéngdū or Lagos (or Dahlen, North Dakota, or in my own neighbourhood in Ottawa, Canada), have downloaded or bought a copy. I can't react to you as I do to my students. You're far away in space, and you're far away in time. Perhaps you're living a century from now and, by some marvellous accident, you find a paper copy in an antique store.

---

1 *Weird*, according to the *Oxford English Dictionary* (online edition, 2020), comes from the Old Norse verb meaning "to become." Its first definition refers to the "principle, power, or agency by which events are predetermined; fate, destiny." What destiny awaits my book? What is its fate?

Perhaps you're the equivalent of what I'd think of as an anthropologist, but you live in a distant solar system, and long after my own sun has died, you capture a copy of my book sent over radio waves (for reasons I can't imagine), and you're trying to figure out what it says about the people who created it. I really don't know. Writing is an act of releasing one's thoughts into a strange, unpredictable void.

Do you know the weirdest thing about reading? Writers. If you're my student, you can read this book and attend my lectures and ask me questions. You have experience with me that helps you judge whether I'm being sincere or making a joke or getting lost on a tangent, as I often do. That judgment helps you make sense of my argument by providing the context to determine not just what propositions I'm making (how I link one idea to another), but the purpose for which I am making them and how I hope they prompt you to act.[2]

But what if you're not my student? For all you know, I could be lying.[3] Maybe this book is an elaborate prank and I'm a scholar in a different field with an axe to grind about what I see as sloppy work in the humanities. In a different vein, if you are far away and do not share my cultural references or sense of humour, maybe my silly asides seem serious and my serious points silly. If you're an alien anthropologist, maybe I use different words than you (even accounting for whatever translation my book must undergo for you to read it), and you can't tell if I mean the same thing you would mean if you wrote the words I'm writing.

The difference between speaking and writing is in the nature of the event that each act brings about. For Paul Ricoeur, what defines speaking—what makes it an *event*—is that it is fleeting, realized temporally and in the present. It occurs in a specific place and is *about* something: speakers refer to the world around them and to

---

2 In other words, our presence together in a room gives you the tools you need to determine what J. L. Austin calls the locutionary, illocutionary, and perlocutionary dimensions of my speech. Austin, *How to Do Things with Words*, 120.

3 Of course, I might be lying even if you are my student, but if you're in the same room with me, you have more clues to use to evaluate my sincerity.

themselves.[4] Hence, during a lecture, I can adjust course if needs be, clarifying my intention as I evaluate my audience's expectations and reactions. I can also refer to current events, or the beautiful trees outside the building where we are meeting, or to shared cultural points of reference.

But when I'm writing, I can't do any of these things. I can anticipate questions that readers might have, and I can play at speaking for both of us, adding rhetorical questions or footnotes to voice the words I imagine they might speak, but I can't adjust course or clarify my intentions if I've misjudged readers' reactions. As soon as I commit my words to paper, nothing prevents my readers— or you, whoever you are—from interpreting my words in ways I can't predict.[5]

What makes different interpretations possible is the inherent polysemy of language (from the Greek πολυ or *poly*, meaning "many," and σῆμα or *sêma*, meaning "sign"). Because we both understand English (you are reading this book, after all), we share a common set of words that allow us to exchange ideas, but that exchange is never perfect. We have both encountered any given word in different circumstances, which colour the associations it evokes for me or for you: when I use a word, I take into account the circumstances in which I've used it before, as do you. As a result, it evokes a different chain of associations for each of us, in ways that I as a writer can neither predict nor control. When we're talking face-to-face, I can actively

---

4 Paul Ricoeur, *Hermeneutics and the Human Sciences: Essays on Language, Action and Interpretation*, 95. He is responding here to structural linguists following lines laid out in Ferdinand de Saussure's *Cours de linguistique générale* (published in English as the *Course in General Linguistics*), whose main interest lay in the system that made reference to the world possible, but not the act of reference itself.

5 Let me take this observation one step further. I'll make revisions to my manuscript based on feedback I get in my seminar next fall, crafting this book, as I have done with earlier books, as if it were a turn taken in a conversation. But it isn't exactly, as my reference to "next fall" makes clear. That reference will be obsolete by the time this book is published because my present is—will be?—your past.

intervene to influence how you interpret what I say, but when you're reading my written words, I can't.[6]

Given the divergent nature of speaking and writing, can discourse take the form of an event in *written* form? In contrast to conversation, the exchange that takes place through writing is not fleeting, nor does it necessarily occur in a specific place. (As I write, I'm sitting in my basement in Ottawa. As you read, where are you?) Although a written exchange might be about something in common, the participants probably do not share an immediate environment to refer to, and they can refer to each other only in the awkward, open-ended ways I've tried describing you, my unknown reader.

And yet, written language, too, can become an event, through metaphor, text, and, most broadly, meaningful action, whenever they reveal a new world that a reader or interpreter comes to appropriate. Each of these terms—metaphor, text, meaningful action, world, appropriate—requires explanation. This chapter focuses on the first three as a way to begin to approach the latter two. To make sense of metaphors, texts, and meaningful actions, we first have to accept that they are obdurate, stubborn things that resist our efforts to impose meaning on them. Otherwise, we will fail to see the challenge they pose by showing where we are wrong. We will read them but, like students moving through the rote motions of reading the syllabus on the first day of class, we will learn nothing. No exchange will have taken place.

If, on the other hand, we use the exchange they make possible to relinquish our old notions of the world, we can find meaning in them. To find meaning in this way—a simultaneous act of giving up and claiming anew—is appropriation. The act of relinquishing is difficult and disorienting. To see how relinquishing occurs, this chapter explores, first, a long-standing argument about

---

6 Ricoeur, *Hermeneutics and the Human Sciences*, 4. For a more careful analysis of the way our experiences shape the chains of associations that words evoke, see Kyle Conway, *The Art of Communication in a Polarized World*, chap. 1.

whether academic writing in the humanities and social sciences is bad, along with the moral panic that such writing has engendered. Then it explores two texts, Charles Dickens's *A Christmas Carol*, and an episode of the TV show *Star Trek: Voyager*, to see how this disorientation feels. We'll let those texts instruct us so we can discover just what it means to say that, when we first encounter a text, to read—that is, to open ourselves to the world a text sets before us—is to feel lost.

Metaphor, Text, and Meaningful Action

The introductory chapter is about metaphor, and here I've added text and meaningful action—similar objects, but on different scales. A text is likely the most familiar: it is longer than a sentence, has a fixed form, and is open to interpretation.[7] A metaphor, as the last chapter hinted at, is a text "in miniature."[8] The category of meaningful action is the most abstract: it describes the actions people take that, within the context of the rules that structure social interaction, are imbued with meaning. In this respect, metaphor, text, and meaningful action are telescoping terms: although they are not identical, insights provided by one help us understand the others, but on different scales. (This effect is what I was referring to in the introductory chapter when I said that the exchange of messages takes the structure of a metaphor. In the concluding chapter, we'll add another term—other people—when we ask what the paradoxical process of appropriation can reveal about our interactions with others.)

Let's consider what the category of the text helps us see about metaphor (text on a micro-scale) and meaningful action (text on a

---

7 Ricoeur, *Hermeneutics and the Human Sciences*, 98.

8 Ricoeur, *Hermeneutics and the Human Sciences*, 129. Elsewhere Ricoeur describes a metaphor as a "poem in miniature," a description I like better. Ricoeur, *The Rule of Metaphor: The Creation of Meaning in Language*, 109.

macro-scale) (table 2). One of the defining features of a text is that its content makes propositional claims. In other words, it says, in varying degrees of complexity, that X is Y or A does B. But its content is fixed, and when readers encounter it, authors are not present to clarify their intention. Not only that, but the audience for a text is potentially limitless: it is available to anyone who can read it. In this way, texts are distanced from their authors, whose intention ceases to provide the scale by which "correct" interpretations are measured. In fact, a text's unruly polysemy—the way it allows for competing plausible interpretations—renders authors' intentions largely unknowable.[9] To what, then, do their propositional claims refer? According to Ricoeur, because they can't refer to a shared environment (their references are "non-ostensive," to use his technical term),[10] they make their own world. As abstract as this idea sounds, it's a common enough experience, especially in fiction. Think of how J. K. Rowling creates the world of Harry Potter or J. R. R. Tolkien the world of Middle-earth. All texts make a world, and the reader's task is to discern it.

Metaphors function in a similar way. They make propositional claims ("The sea is like wine"), and, once made, the comparison constitutes the metaphor. Its form is fixed. The author's intention remains inaccessible, leaving readers—who could be anyone—to interpret a metaphor by exploring how its figurative meaning goes beyond its literal meaning.[11] The same is true of meaningful action. The things people do are meaningful to the degree that other people interpret them. (You've interpreted actions any time you've tried to

---

9 Even if an author were to write, "My intention in this text was to _____," that description would be subject to the same limitations as the text the author was trying to explain. The author might explain the intention behind their statement of intention, but in the end this recursive logic keeps the author's intention always out of reach.

10 Ricoeur, *Hermeneutics and the Human Sciences*, 103.

11 Ricoeur, *Rule of Metaphor*, chaps. 3, 6, and 7, and "Metaphor and the Main Problem of Hermeneutics."

Table 2. Metaphor, text, and meaningful action as forms of discourse

	Metaphor	Text	Meaningful action
Content makes propositional claims	A metaphor says "this is like that"	A text makes claims about the world	Actions bear meaning, e.g., about cause/effect or relationships
Content is fixed	Once made, the comparison constitutes the metaphor	A text is written (in a broad sense of "writing")	An action "leaves a mark"
Author's intention is distant	Readers make connections, produce meanings	An author is not present to clarify their intention	Actors are not present to explain their intentions
Audience is potentially limitless	A metaphor can be interpreted by anyone	A text can be read by anyone	Actions can be interpreted by anyone
World referred to is not that of immediate environment	The metaphorical meaning goes beyond the literal meaning	A text refers to a world of its own making	People interpret actions in new contexts

Sources: Ricoeur, *The Rule of Metaphor*, chaps. 3, 6, and 7, and *Hermeneutics and the Human Sciences*, chaps. 4–8.

explain why someone did something.) An action's content is fixed, so to speak, through a type of inscription: "We say that such-and-such event *left its mark* on its time," explains Ricoeur: "We speak of marking events."[12] (Think of the way the attacks of September 11, 2001, marked world politics, or how they affected people's individual and collective understandings of their relationships to strangers.) The actors, like the authors of a text, are not necessarily present to explain their intentions, which are open to interpretation by anyone observing the actions, either as they happen or, more likely,

---

12 Ricoeur, *Hermeneutics and the Human Sciences*, 167, original emphasis.

retrospectively. And as time passes, people interpret them in new contexts, outside the shared environment where they took place. They, too, make non-ostensive reference to a new world.[13]

What we are beginning to see is that to understand a text is to enter into the world it creates through its propositional claims. Put another way, to read like you mean it is to explore the world made by a text. Ricoeur calls this *appropriation*, a term he uses to describe the work one undertakes "'to make one's own' what was initially 'alien',," which "takes the place of the answer in the dialogical situation."[14] In that respect, it's what has the potential to constitute written discourse as an event. But it is a paradoxical act because in order to explore a text's new world, readers must give up the idea that their own world, by which I mean the sum total of their ideas about their identity and their relationships to others, is stable or complete. They exchange certainty in their own situation for something new and risky: the world of the text, if it is compelling enough, reconfigures their understanding of themselves.

In this way, appropriation acts as the counterpart to the distanciation across time and space that puts the author's intention out of reach. Readers interpret a metaphor or text, or observers interpret an action, making an argument about what it means, but other people can interpret the same metaphor, text, or action differently. People must defend their interpretations against those of others, and as a result, their act of appropriation becomes "not so much a possession of the world around us as a *dispossession* of the certainty with which we might presume to understand" the world—or a text within it.[15] In other words, in order to defend their interpretation, people must see it as others see it, stepping outside

---

13 Ricoeur, *Hermeneutics and the Human Sciences*, 165–70.

14 Ricoeur, *Hermeneutics and the Human Sciences*, 147. In some contexts, such as North America, *appropriation* is a potentially misleading term, suggesting the act of taking something unjustly, as in the case of cultural appropriation. Note that Ricoeur does not use it this way.

15 Sarah Maitland, *What Is Cultural Translation?* 139.

of themselves—distancing themselves from the world they take for granted—in order to see themselves as others do.[16]

But I'm getting ahead of myself. The experiences that accompany this process are as important as the process itself (they become a lens through which to observe our reading strategies), and I have said nothing about them yet. They will be the focus of the rest of this chapter and then the three chapters that follow. I've observed in my own experience of reading, not to mention that of my students, that one place where people often stop is at the beginning because they feel anxious about the disorientation a difficult text causes. They feel lost in the face of what I described in the introductory chapter as the "literal *is not*," or the confounding nature of the text's literal meaning, which leads to confusion because its component parts—the things it says—appear to contradict each other or what we think we know.

But as I'll show here, the feeling of being lost can become positive if we find ways to harness it. When we feel that what we're reading is more than we can comprehend, we need to wander a bit to establish a new perspective (the focus of chapter 2). When we do, there's a moment of excitement or euphoria, as what we're reading gives us a new way to think about the world (chapter 3), although we must find ways not to let our euphoria get the better of us. We are still tethered to the text, whose form does not change, but we can find a new freedom in the space between it and the world it opens up (chapter 4).

Fear and Distanciation

Halfway through his book *How to Do Things with Words*, J. L. Austin makes a useful observation for our discussion here. He is trying—and failing, albeit deliberately—to use grammatical forms to devise a way to distinguish between sentences that merely *say* something

---

16 Ricoeur, *Hermeneutics and the Human Sciences*, 97–103. See also Kyle Conway, "The Vicissitudes of Untranslatability."

and sentences that *do* the things they say, the way "I name this ship the *Queen Elizabeth*," spoken by the right person in the right circumstances, officially christens a ship.[17] His purpose is to challenge philosophers' and linguists' fundamental notions of how language works. He tries one way, which fails, then another way, which also fails, until he arrives at a point where, in a parenthetical aside, he admits, "I must explain again that we are floundering here. To feel the firm ground of prejudice slipping away is exhilarating, but it brings its revenges."[18] In these two sentences, he captures the tension between the fear we feel when we discover that what we thought we knew was actually a hindrance and the exhilaration we experience when we read something that causes us to see the world in new ways. In effect, he suggests a way to approach distanciation and its effects on readers obliquely, through the disorientation and fear we feel when we read difficult texts.

I suggested in the introductory chapter that some texts make us feel confused or angry when we read them. A more succinct way to say the same thing is that they *negate* us: they seem to tell us (or we take them as evidence) that we are not capable enough, not smart enough—not, not, *not*.[19] Certain authors and fields are especially controversial in this respect. Over the course of the last two decades, there has been an acrimonious debate in particular about writing in the human sciences, a term I am using to designate both humanities

---

17 J. L. Austin, *How to Do Things with Words*, 5.

18 Austin, *How to Do Things with Words*, 61.

19 This is another symptom of the "literal *is not*." Consider this book's epigraph, six lines from one of Rainer Maria Rilke's best known sonnets, known in English as "The Archaic Torso of Apollo." The poem is about the world the narrator imagines while staring at a fragment of a statue of Apollo. The world draws the narrator in, but then the poem issues a command in its dramatic final line: *Du mußt dein Leben ändern*—"You must change your life." Why did I leave these lines in German, if the rest of the book is in English? To emphasize the distance between it and the reader: at the linguistic level, it pushes readers away, while at that of content, it invites them in. Why did I omit the final dramatic line? To invite readers to fill it in themselves—to pass from the "literal *is not*" to the "metaphorical *is*."

and social sciences.[20] In the mid-1990s, Dennis Dutton, editor of the journal *Philosophy and Literature*, sponsored the Bad Writing Contest to draw attention to what he saw as "the most egregious examples of awkward, jargon-clogged academic prose from all over the English-speaking world."[21] Poor writing, he thought, was really just a sign of sloppy thinking, and it was endemic to fields such as English, cultural studies, sociology, and anthropology that, in his view, tried to elevate trivial topics as part of a cynical ploy to increase enrolments in fields that students found old and stodgy. "No one denies the need for a specialized vocabulary in biochemistry or physics or in technical areas of the humanities like linguistics," he wrote in a *Wall Street Journal* article about the contest. "But among literature professors who do what they now call 'theory'—mostly inept philosophy applied to literature and culture—jargon has become the emperor's clothing of choice" (figure 3).[22] He made the idea of negation explicit: "If readers are baffled by a phrase like 'disclosing the absentation of actuality'"—drawn from Paul Fry's *A Defense of Poetry*—"they will imagine it's due to their own ignorance."[23] In response to the sentence by Judith Butler that "won" the contest in 1999, he says, "This sentence beats readers into submission and instructs them that they are in the presence of a great and deep mind. Actual communication has nothing to do with it."[24]

---

20 The term *human sciences* is not as common in English as *sciences humaines* is in French. Here I'm borrowing it from Ricoeur, who explores *les sciences humaines* extensively. He, in turn, is borrowing largely from the German Romantics, who used the term *Geisteswissenschaften*. Although one way to translate *sciences humaines* might be "the humanities," it has a more expansive meaning. The tradition of the human sciences emphasizes questions of method, understanding, and critique, in ways that go beyond the humanities in the English-speaking world. See Kurt Mueller-Vollmer, "Language, Mind, and Artifact: An Outline of Hermeneutic Theory Since the Enlightenment."

21 Dennis Dutton, "Language Crimes: A Lesson in How Not to Write, Courtesy of the Professoriate."

22 Dutton, "Language Crimes."

23 Dutton, "Language Crimes."

24 Dutton, "Language Crimes."

Figure 3. "Jargon has become the emperor's clothing of choice."
Source: Modified from *Alasti keiser*, stencil graffiti by Edward
von Lõngus, image by Ivo Kruusamägi. Wikimedia Commons.

His was not the only salvo. At the same time as Dutton was
running the Bad Writing Contest, Alan Sokal, a physicist and math-
ematician, pulled off the biggest academic hoax in the last half
century. Like Dutton, he thought that jargon-laden writing in the
human sciences served to hide sloppy thinking, but he went still

further, accusing the authors of such works of being more motivated by ideology than rigorous thought. To make his point, he submitted an article to *Social Text*, a journal that was a standard-bearer of the type of scholarship he wanted to challenge. *Social Text* published the article, called "Transgressing the Boundaries: Towards a Transformative Hermeneutics of Quantum Gravity," in its spring-summer 1996 issue. In it, Sokal argued that gravity was merely a social construction, not something real that everyone experienced, an idea that he claimed advanced "progressive" political goals. After it was published, he revealed in another publication, *Lingua Franca*, that it was a hoax meant to answer the question, "Would a leading North American journal of cultural studies—whose editorial collective includes such luminaries as Fredric Jameson and Andrew Ross—publish an article liberally salted with nonsense if (*a*) it sounded good and (*b*) it flattered the editors' ideological preconceptions?"[25] The answer was yes, he said, despite the fact that he wrote the article to be an "annotated bibliography of the charlatanism and nonsense purveyed by dozens of prominent French and American intellectuals."[26] The editors disputed his accusation that their criterion for acceptance was ideology rather than rigour, although they also described the article, in a form of a posteriori rationalization, as an apparently clumsy attempt by an author they perceived as well-meaning who was trying to think outside his normal framework.[27] Their response had little effect on the ensuing debate, during which Sokal's supporters did not hide their glee in revealing what they saw as the vapid pseudo-intellectualism of scholars beholden only to their "progressive" ideological dogma.[28]

25 Alan Sokal, "A Physicist Experiments with Cultural Studies."

26 Sokal, writing in response to the journal's editors Bruce Robbins and Andrew Ross in "Mystery Science Theater."

27 Robbins and Ross, "Mystery Science Theater."

28 See Evelyn Fox Keller, Steven Fuller, Paul Boghossian, Thomas Nagel, Franco Moretti, Ellen Schrecker, Peter Caws, Teri Reynolds, David Layton, Lee Smolin, and George Levine, "The Sokal Hoax: A Forum."

Nor did the debate end with Sokal's article. Indeed, two decades later, Helen Pluckrose, James A. Lindsay, and Peter Boghossian produced a series of articles to submit to a range of journals, their goal being to demonstrate that Sokal's trick would still work.[29] They cut with a sharper knife. Whereas Sokal later argued that he wanted, ultimately, to strengthen humanities research by encouraging scholars to abandon the "currently fashionable postmodernist/poststructuralist/social-constructivist discourse,"[30] Pluckrose and her colleagues wanted to tear down whole fields of studies, such as cultural studies and women's studies, that they (along with legions of conservative political commentators) derided as "grievance studies."

Of course, *Social Text* had its defenders, as do the fields attacked by Sokal's imitators two decades later. Stanley Fish, for instance, accused Sokal of acting in bad faith and misunderstanding his main philosophical target, the idea of socially constructed reality. Something can be socially constructed *and* real, he argued, and to see philosophers (and sociologists) of science—Sokal's main institutional targets—as rivals was to miss the point that they were undertaking a very different type of enterprise. They were not doing science but trying to understand *how* science was done.[31]

Addressing the question of "bad" writing more directly, some scholars have argued that everyone uses jargon and that even what appear to be clear statements can be explained, interpreted, or otherwise rephrased.[32] For that reason, taking sentences out of context, as the sponsors of the Bad Writing Contest did, is also an act of bad faith, one to which the critics of "bad" writing can be subjected,

---

29 Helen Pluckrose, James A. Lindsay, and Peter Boghossian, "Academic Grievance Studies and the Corruption of Scholarship."

30 Alan D. Sokal, "Transgressing the Boundaries: An Afterword," 339. Note that this afterword was published in Dutton's journal, *Philosophy and Literature*.

31 Stanley Fish, "Professor Sokal's Bad Joke."

32 Jan Mieszkowski, "Here Come the Prose Police." The second part of this statement—that everything can be interpreted—is also a clear statement of one of the key points of *How to Read Like You Mean It*.

too.[33] A humanities scholar who uses difficult language is "not pretending to be a journalist," according to Joan Scott, and to attack such scholars for bad writing is nothing more than "a kind of anti-intellectualism that is everywhere in the culture, a demand for things they already agree with."[34]

The "winners" of the Bad Writing Contest also addressed the theme of anti-intellectualism. Common sense, Judith Butler responded, is pernicious because it is entrenched in ordinary language, and it takes difficult language to express difficult ideas that break free of this trap.[35] (Not coincidentally, she points out, scholars attacked for bad writing are also often those trying to challenge the common-sense status quo.) Difficult writing results from the process of working through complex ideas, as Edward Said explained with respect to another "winner," Homi Bhabha, because writers are aware of how language and thought influence each other and how words always evoke more than authors intend.[36] For this reason, difficult writing stands as a bulwark against the homogenizing tendencies of the university-turned-job-training-centre.[37]

The Bad Writing Contest and the Sokal hoax (and its imitators) are useful here as an illustration. I'm not interested in the twists and turns of the decades-long debate that they provoked, other than to say that to read through the many exchanges now is to witness a conversation—if that term applies at all—where the participants talk past each other while insisting that they understand each other perfectly well, thank you very much. Instead, these debates suggest three possible ways to understand the feeling that readers have

---

33 Mieszkowski, "Here Come the Prose Police."

34 Quoted in Dinitia Smith, "When Ideas Get Lost in Bad Writing."

35 Judith Butler, "A 'Bad Writer' Bites Back."

36 Quoted in Smith, "When Ideas Get Lost in Bad Writing." Note how Said's position is consistent with the one I have adopted in the first half of this chapter.

37 Jacques Lezra, *Untranslating Machines: A Genealogy for the Ends of Global Thought*; Anthony Alessandrini, "Against 'Critical Thinking': Are We Giving Students the Right Tools?"; Conway, "The Vicissitudes of Untranslatability."

when they encounter a text they don't understand. The first two are forms of negation. Difficult texts (or metaphors or meaningful actions) seem first to negate them as readers: they are not smart enough to understand them. Dutton and Sokal, on the other hand, seem to negate entire fields: authors are hiding the fact that they have nothing to say. Finally, the defenders of "bad" writing offer an explanation that doesn't take the form of a negation: authors are wrestling with the task of expressing complex ideas.

One of the challenges readers face is that although there are three possible reasons they don't understand these texts, by virtue of the very fact they don't understand them, they can't even determine which of the possibilities is correct. (If they understood them, then they could tell whether authors had something to say or not, and whether, as a result, they were in fact smart enough to judge them for themselves.) They're a bit like the hapless pilot whose flying machine has collapsed in figure 4: they've lost their points of reference, and they're floundering, to return to Austin. They "feel the firm ground of prejudice slipping away," which may be "exhilarating," but more than anything, they are aware of "its revenges."[38]

One possibility that these debates leave largely unexplored is that people can learn to read difficult texts. If they do, they can also learn how to evaluate them and then decide for themselves which of the three possibilities suggested by the debates is the most plausible. In that respect, the negation they experience is valuable because it is a symptom of a greater interpretive uneasiness they experience when faced with any text (or metaphor or meaningful action). It is a result of their distanciation from a text. They cannot say with certainty "This text means _____" because their claim can be challenged, no

---

38 Austin, *How to Do Things with Words*, 61. Note how the image in the figure acts as a metaphor, as I compare readers to the balloonist. Does the comparison tell you something about the experience of reading? Perhaps it is such a weird comparison that you're thinking, "I don't get it." What happens if you let go of your expectations (gained from your past experience) about reading? How does this metaphor change your ideas, even if slightly?

Figure 4. As readers, we are sometimes like this hapless pilot when, suddenly, we are falling into the void. Source: Auguste Trichon, *Flying Man Vincent de Groof Falling Down* (1887). OldBookIllustrations.com.

matter how they fill in the blank. Nor can they appeal to the author's intention, which is lost to them. All they can do is appeal to—and defend—their own understanding, which is always coloured by a certain degree of doubt. I'll say more about this doubt in chapters 3 and 4 when I talk about the paradox of appropriation, but for now,

I'm counting on the fact that you, too, have had this experience of bewilderment or frustration, where it feels like you're falling through the void.

Falling Through the Void

If you haven't, then I'm counting on the fact that you can imagine the experience. Literature and popular culture can help. Stories abound of people falling through the void, and here I propose to examine two. The first, Charles Dickens's *A Christmas Carol*, is well known, while the second, an episode of *Star Trek: Voyager* called "Barge of the Dead," will be best known among the science fiction-loving demographic that includes me. I could choose others, but these illustrate the experience I want to discuss in ways that help us see facets of reading that might not otherwise be clear.

What I'm proposing to do, in effect, is to interpret these stories in ways that differ from how others have responded to them but remain nonetheless grounded in their specific propositional claims and the worlds they open up.[39] What makes this approach possible is the fact of distanciation, as described above. (I mean, what are the authors going to do—tell me I'm wrong?) In this way, I use these stories as metaphors for interpretation. They reveal something novel about the dialectic of distanciation and appropriation, although to say that readers before a text are like Ebenezer Scrooge before the Ghost of Christmas Yet to Come, or like B'Elanna Torres on the Klingon Barge of the Dead, doesn't mean that readers can be reduced to either of those characters in their respective situations. Instead, these comparisons invite us to see the act of reading through different lenses, which reveal aspects of reading that were not as clear before. The tension linking the components of my metaphors arises from the

---

39 With respect to this approach, see Conway, *The Art of Communication in a Polarized World*, 17–23.

fact that these stories are polysemic, always possessing potential new readings, and I am consequently obligated to justify my interpretation in light of your potential challenges. My justification is grounded in the idea that what we see in these relationships, if my metaphors are any good, might compel us to think about reading in a new way.

Charles Dickens's A Christmas Carol

Of the two stories I want to examine, Charles Dickens's *A Christmas Carol* is undoubtedly the better known. It was first published in 1843 and has been adapted many times since. (The 1984 television adaptation starring George C. Scott left an indelible mark on my childhood.) The story is that of Ebenezer Scrooge, a miserly businessman in Victorian England. The ghost of his dead partner Jacob Marley visits him on Christmas Eve to warn him that he will be visited by three spirits. Marley tells him he must change his ways, but of course Scrooge resists. (There would be no plot if he simply acquiesced!) He is visited by three ghosts in turn—the Ghost of Christmas Past, the Ghost of Christmas Present, and the Ghost of Christmas Yet to Come—who show him scenes of himself when he was younger and happier (but also when he lost the woman he loved because she distracted him from business), scenes of his family and that of his employee Bob Cratchit celebrating Christmas in the present, and finally, scenes of a dark future. It is those last scenes of Christmas Yet to Come that are my interest here.

The visit from the Ghost of Christmas Yet to Come occurs in the fourth chapter (or "stave," as Dickens calls it) of *A Christmas Carol*. All of the prior ghosts have spoken to Scrooge, but when the last one appears, it is mute. Instead, it leads Scrooge through the streets of London, where he witnesses a series of conversations about an unnamed dead man. First he sees merchants talking at the Exchange about the man's death; they say they'll go to his funeral only if lunch is served. Then he sees two men in a crowd talking indifferently about the man's death. Scrooge looks for himself in the crowd, but he is not there. In fact, although most readers likely suspect that the dead man is Scrooge himself, he remains wilfully blind to that possibility.

The ghost then takes Scrooge to an unfamiliar part of the city, where the "ways were foul and narrow; the shops and houses wretched; the people half-naked, drunken, slipshod, ugly."[40] He sees a man buying items stolen from the dead man's room, and he thinks they look like things he owns. He even comments, "The case of this unhappy man might be my own,"[41] without recognizing, of course, that it is. Even when the ghost takes him to the room where the body lies—*his* room—he does not realize who is beneath the sheets.

In effect, Scrooge is floundering. He is lost, but because he cannot fathom that the dead man might be him, he cannot read the evidence before him. But his anxiety increases with each new scene, as the images chip away at his confidence in his conception of the world. Eager to sense human connection, he asks to see someone who feels something other than indifference about this man's death, and the ghost shows him a poor couple who feel relieved because their "merciless" creditor is no more.[42] He asks to see someone who has feelings of warmth, and the ghost shows him his employee Bob Cratchit, whose son Tiny Tim has died. Even then, Scrooge asks, "Tell me what man that was whom we saw lying dead?"[43] Still, as the ghost takes him to the cemetery, when they pass his old office, he asks to see himself to "behold what I shall be, in days to come!"[44]

It is only when they reach the cemetery and the ghost points to a specific grave that he begins to realize who it is that has died. His panic sets in, and he demands, "Are these shadows of the things that

---

40 Charles Dickens, *A Christmas Carol*, 105.

41 Dickens, *A Christmas Carol*, 111.

42 Dickens, *A Christmas Carol*, 114.

43 Dickens, *A Christmas Carol*, 120.

44 Dickens, *A Christmas Carol*, 120.

will be, or are they shadows of things that may be, only?"[45] As he reads the tombstone, he experiences the most literal of negations: he learns he is no more. He has died. Up to this point, he has protested that he has learned his lesson and will heed Marley's warning, but it is only now, as he sees his grave, that he demonstrates that he knows what that task will entail. In contrast to his prior impatient (and insincere) protests, he now pleads: "Spirit! . . . hear me! I am not the man I was. I will not be the man I must have been but for this intercourse. Why show me this, if I am past all hope!"[46] He is relinquishing control, seeing what he had refused to see, and the ghost's hand, steady until now as it pointed the way, begins to shake. Scrooge interprets the tremor as the ghost's acknowledgement that it will intercede on his behalf. Scrooge's words show how his world has now been reconfigured:

> I will honour Christmas in my heart, and try to keep it all the year. I will live in the past, the present, and the future. The spirits of all three shall strive within me. I will not shut out the lessons that they teach. Oh, tell me I may sponge away the writing on this stone![47]

Scrooge's evolution is suggestive where the nature of reading and interpretation is concerned. Although the stakes are not as high for readers, the feeling of floundering is real. We bring our expectations to a text, but often the text does not follow them and it won't yield. I know I've had the experience where I struggle to find an author's argument because my preconceived ideas about the object of study block my ability to see what the author is actually saying. Perhaps even now you're thinking to yourself, "But I already know how to read! I don't get the big deal about Charles Dickens. What's that got to do with anything, anyway?" My challenge as a writer is to use

---

45 Dickens, *A Christmas Carol*, 121.

46 Dickens, *A Christmas Carol*, 122.

47 Dickens, *A Christmas Carol*, 122.

Dickens to convince you that what you think you know about reading is actually getting in your way.

Star Trek: Voyager, *"Barge of the Dead"*

"Barge of the Dead" was the third episode of the sixth season of *Star Trek: Voyager*, the fifth series of the *Star Trek* franchise. The series itself told the story of a starship called *Voyager*, thrown so far off course that it would take decades to return to Earth. "Barge of the Dead" focused on the ship's chief engineer, B'Elanna Torres, whose father was human and mother was Klingon, an alien species that valued honour earned through valour in war. Over the first five seasons, B'Elanna, angry that her mother left her father when she was a child, has fought to dominate the traits of her personality that she finds to be too Klingon.

"Barge of the Dead" begins when B'Elanna returns to *Voyager* on a shuttle craft, having come through an ion storm that disabled her navigation controls. Viewers later learn that she was unconscious when she arrived and that her memory of the crash landing came from the fever dream that serves as the episode's conceit. (The things that happen to her mark her because she does not know they are a dream. They feel real.) As her fever dream progresses, she finds herself on the Barge of the Dead, which transports Klingons without honour to Gre'thor, the Klingon version of hell. There she finds her mother Miral, who is being sent to Gre'thor because B'Elanna, by rejecting her Klingon identity, has brought her dishonour. B'Elanna performs a ritual to take her mother's place, but the ritual fails, and her mother returns to the barge.

B'Elanna's immediate goal of saving her mother and her long-standing goal of repudiating her Klingon traits are clearly in conflict. Her approach, in particular her desire to exert control over her identity and the course of her life, is what makes the episode a useful tool for thinking about the act of interpretation. In the episode's climactic scene, B'Elanna confronts her mother and asks why she has come back:

B'ELANNA: I don't understand.

MIRAL: You never did.

B'ELANNA: I did everything that the ritual told me to do. I came back for you—

MIRAL: Forget the ritual. It's meaningless.

B'ELANNA: Meaningless? I died for you!

MIRAL: No, you didn't. It's not your time. You still don't understand this journey.

B'ELANNA: Then tell me!

MIRAL: Request denied.[48]

The remarkable thing about this exchange is the way it links confusion and negation. "I don't understand," B'Elanna says. Her mother's response includes two forms of negation: first, she says the ritual had no meaning, and second, she refuses to tell B'Elanna what she wants to know. The exchange puts into words the experience readers have when they encounter a difficult text: they are confused, and when they plead for an explanation, the text does not readily yield one up.

After this exchange, B'Elanna begins to flounder. "What do you want?" she demands of her mother. "Who are you asking?" Miral replies. B'Elanna lists everyone she can think of: "You! Kahless![49] The tooth fairy! Anybody who will tell me what I'm supposed to do!"[50] Soon, her friends from *Voyager* appear to surround her. She demands of each in turn, "Tell me what you want me to be! A good Starfleet officer? A good Maquis?[51] Lover? Daughter? Just tell me what you want from me!"[52] Their responses, too, take the form of negation, in particular when Tuvok, the security chief, and Tom Paris, the bad-boy pilot and B'Elanna's boyfriend, advance on her, saying, "Defend

48 Ronald D. Moore and Bryan Fuller, *Star Trek: Voyager*, "Barge of the Dead," 39:33–39:56.

49 Founder of the Klingon empire.

50 Moore and Fuller, "Barge of the Dead," 39:57–40:07.

51 The Maquis were a rebel group to which B'Elanna belonged before ending up on *Voyager*.

52 Moore and Fuller, "Barge of the Dead," 41:07–41:23.

yourself." At that point, she stops. "I don't know how," she says. "I'm so tired of fighting." She then throws the weapon she is holding into the stormy sea before collapsing.[53] Something has changed, and her mother congratulates her: "You have taken the first step of your journey."[54]

Although the presentation is ham-fisted (like most commercial programs that strive for gravitas), what it suggests about the distanciation and appropriation is no less valuable. Up until this point, B'Elanna has tried—and failed—to exert control over her situation by imposing upon it her understanding of what she thinks it should be. When she actively rejects her Klingon traits, or when she demands that others tell her what to do, she holds fast to the idea that she can control her own fate. In a similar way, when readers come to difficult texts and try to fit them into their preconceptions about the world, they are similarly frustrated. Just as B'Elanna's mother and shipmates do not yield, the texts do not yield. It is only when B'Elanna relinquishes control, when she throws her weapon overboard, allowing her shipmates to tell her things that will reconfigure the symbolic world through which she moves, that she is able to understand what they have to tell her. Her floundering leads her to give up her preconceived ideas and trying to impose her interpretation of the situation on the situation itself, but in giving up, she finds part of the meaning she is looking for.

I will leave you to draw the relevant conclusions about reading and interpretation.

Conclusion: To Read Is to Feel Lost

"Come on," you say, now that we've reached the end of the chapter. "That's ridiculous. Dickens was writing about Christmas, and the

---

53 Moore and Fuller, "Barge of the Dead," 41:30–41:47.
54 Moore and Fuller, "Barge of the Dead," 42:02–42:04.

writers for *Voyager* were just trying to attract viewers so the network could get a good price for ads. They're just stories. Why are you reading into them?"

"Okay," I say. "Let's find the writers and ask them. Do you have their phone number?"

I admit—I'm being cheeky. Maybe you say that only in my imagination. Maybe you've bought my argument. I am no more capable of knowing your reaction than you are of contacting Charles Dickens. It's this fact that authorizes my apparent flight of interpretive fancy.

But to be clear, I'm not claiming that my reading of these stories, or of the controversies about "bad" writing in the human sciences, is authoritative. When I'm interpreting texts (Dickens or *Voyager* here, the biblical books of Exodus and Numbers in chapter 2, Plato's *Phaedrus* or Sappho's Fragment 31 in chapter 3, and so on), I'm not asking "What does this mean?" Instead I'm asking, "What does this reveal about the *experience* of reading?" The texts I have chosen affect us at an emotional level, and it's at that level that we come to know what it is to read like you mean it. It's a different type of knowing—visceral rather than cerebral, but also leading inductively to an intellectual understanding of this process.

I also want to show that written discourse, like its spoken counterpart, can become an event. Although the content of metaphors, texts, and meaningful actions is fixed, something happens in my *encounter* with them. They bring about a change, and that change is fleeting, occurs in a specific place, and refers to a world I come to share with the text (even if I cannot point to that world in the same way I point to objects in my Ottawa basement, where I like to write). This is how appropriation, which we've only just begun to explore, becomes a turn taken in a conversation, made possible by our recognition of the ways we flounder and, consequently, give up control.

Before we explore appropriation further, however, we must first discuss the ways we find perspective when we're falling through the void. That is the topic of the next chapter.

2

To Read Is to Wander

Here's a scenario that will be easy to imagine, depending on where you are and when you're reading this. It's March 2020, and a novel coronavirus—like the kind that causes the cold, but deadlier and more contagious—is disrupting life the world over. It started spreading in China, then ravaged Europe, and is now upturning lives in North America. (It will soon move on to South America, but there's no way to know that yet.) It is highly contagious, but because people don't show symptoms for the first two weeks, it is hard to control. The most effective approach is for everyone to stay at home, away from everyone else, in hopes of interrupting person-to-person transmission. Cities, states, provinces, and countries shut down, but no one knows for how long. People miss their family and friends and long for human contact. They stop buying things as supply chains break down, while schools and workplaces close. As confinement drags on, everyone asks, what will the world look like when it opens up again? How will life change?

What they really want to know is what these changes *mean*: these are the questions people ask when they want to interpret a text or meaningful action, to return to the terms from the last chapter. My scenario isn't hypothetical, of course—at least not to me. I'm writing in mid-June 2020, and because of the COVID-19 pandemic, caused by a virus that started circulating at the end of 2019, the province where I live has been closed since March. Everywhere I look, people are asking these questions. Just the previous week,[1] for instance, a *New York Times* columnist asked what the pandemic will mean for universities in the United States. Will they continue their shift away from the humanities toward science, technology, engineering, and math (STEM)? Will their emphasis on STEM push them further in the direction of job-training as they seek to fulfill the needs of technology companies that promise to produce jobs? Will they continue the trend of devaluing the humanities, even as the "writers, philosophers, historians . . . chart the social, cultural and political challenges of this pandemic"?[2] To answer these questions is to turn the pandemic into a text: it is leaving a mark, which anyone can interpret. The various actors are not present to explain their decisions, which observers will come to see differently as their own context changes. A person might give one answer now and a different answer in a year or a decade, as the effects of the pandemic become clearer and the stories people tell to explain it evolve.

The truth is that we're driven to ask these questions.[3] I'm sitting in my basement (just as when I wrote the last chapter), dreading the fact I need to buy groceries tomorrow, which I'll do by putting on my homemade mask, standing two metres away from other people, and washing my hands with an obsessive thoroughness I've learned over the past three months. It's still not clear when things in my province will open up, or what they'll look like when they do. I miss the comfort of routine and regularity, and to look for it, those are

---

1 I write "the previous week" as if that phrase will be at all meaningful by the time you read this book.

2 Frank Bruni, "The End of College as We Knew It?"

3 This drive to find meaning also explains the increasing prevalence of conspiracy theories, which arrange the facts at hand in new ways, providing different interpretations of events like the COVID-19 epidemic. They're corrosive, but their appeal is not hard to understand. See Jan-Willem van Prooijen, *The Psychology of Conspiracy Theories*.

the questions I'm asking. Although you, my reader, might know how this pandemic ends, I—at least the version of me writing in 2020—do not.

The feeling of disorientation I described in the last chapter is still all too real. I'm a bit lost.

But this situation is not unique, even if it does make the questions feel more urgent. Instead, it's an amplification of a common experience: we want to make sense of the things that happen to us or the things we do. In the introductory chapter, I referred to this need to find meaning in the context of what Ricoeur calls a metaphor's "ontological vehemence," a term I'll explore again in the book's conclusion. In the next chapter, I'll describe this drive as a form of eros, or, in Sam Rocha's words, "a singular, eternal, and irreducible desire for love: the love of love, the desire for desire, the mad longing for longing, passion for passion itself."[4] It's a force that consumes us: our desire to make meaning is stronger than us.

This chapter is about the tools we have to act on that desire. We are constantly called upon to act, even when the information we have is incomplete. In acting, we begin to get a better sense of where the gaps are in our knowledge, and later, as we reflect on our choices and their consequences, we begin to fill them in. The process is circular and iterative, always imperfect, but always leading us toward a more complete understanding of the world through which we navigate.[5]

The most challenging step is the first. To make sense of an event (or of a difficult text or metaphor, to return to our prior categories), we first have to make a guess that will set in motion a cycle of validation and refinement. We make that guess from a state of disorientation, the driftlessness we experience when we try to make

---

4 Samuel D. Rocha, *Folk Phenomenology: Education, Study, and the Human Person*, 10.

5 This approach is grounded in what I call elsewhere an epistemology of jumping in: we learn to swim by jumping in the pool. We learn to make choices by making choices. Kyle Conway, *The Art of Communication in a Polarized World*, 117–28.

sense of a pandemic whose end we can't yet see or a text whose density (like those of the "winners" of the Bad Writing Contest described in chapter 1) confounds us. Making a guess becomes a way to find our new bearings, but it's unnerving because we have yet to establish the bearings we would normally use to orient our guess. This chapter starts by considering the tools of hermeneutics, or the philosophy of interpretation, before turning to stories of people who are wandering, whether figuratively (as in the case of people trying to make sense of the coronavirus) or literally (as in the case of the Israelites in the biblical books of Exodus and Numbers). The emotional heft of their stories counterbalances the more cerebral account of hermeneutics; together they work to show what it means to read and to wander.

Hermeneutics

As I wrote in the introductory chapter, my first goal in this book is pedagogical. Even if I can't predict who my readers will be, I'm imagining the first version of this book as a series of lectures I'll deliver to students next semester in a course on communication method. I hope others read it, too, but at the time of writing it, I'm addressing it like a letter to my students in the Fall 2020 semester at the University of Ottawa. For that reason, one dimension of the book is performative: I'm *doing* the things that I'm also describing. In effect, this book is an extended exploration of the ideas of Paul Ricoeur as they become relevant to my students (and, I hope, to the other readers I might one day reach).

This section is about Ricoeur's hermeneutics, a term I've avoided up to this point because—my goals being pedagogical—I worried that its obscurity might prompt my students to stop reading. But I can no longer avoid it. For Ricoeur, hermeneutics is "the theory of the operations of understanding in their relation to the interpretation of texts."[6] It is grounded in the act of careful reading—the act I'm called to undertake here—where the text, having escaped the author's control and having been made available to anyone who can read, serves as an anchor. As I discuss below, its anchor function is what makes hermeneutics objective, although Ricoeur means something different by *objective* than the social or natural scientists to whom he is responding.

Kurt Mueller-Vollmer traces the roots of hermeneutics back to Aristotle's *On Interpretation* (or, in Greek, Περὶ Ἑρμηνείας or *Peri Hermeneias*), although, he says, the tradition as we know it did not really begin until the Protestant Reformation.[7] It played—and continues to play—an important role in biblical interpretation. Ricoeur is attentive to religion's role, and his account is performative in much the same way as I want this book to be. He examines the creation story in Genesis, for instance, where he finds two narratives: one of action ("God made . . .") and one of speech ("God said, and there was . . ."). "The first narrative," he says,

> could be said to play the role of tradition and the second of interpretation. What is interesting here is that the interpretation, before being the act of the exegete [that is, the person performing the interpretation], is the act of the text. The relation between tradition and interpretation is a relation internal to the text; for the exegete, to interpret is to place himself in the meaning indicated by the relation of interpretation which the text itself supports.[8]

I'm doing work similar to that of the exegete here: I'm placing myself (and my students) in the "relation of interpretation which the text itself supports," although I'm concerned with Ricoeur's work rather

---

6 Paul Ricoeur, *Hermeneutics and the Human Sciences: Essays on Language, Action and Interpretation*, 3.

7 Kurt Mueller-Vollmer, "Language, Mind, and Artifact: An Outline of Hermeneutic Theory Since the Enlightenment," 1–2.

8 Ricoeur, *Hermeneutics and the Human Sciences*, 124.

than the book of Genesis. (It's worth noting, however, that consideration of religion is part of the DNA of communication studies in the United States, where I was trained. It's clear in the work of John Durham Peters and James Carey, for instance, not to mention my own work, as in the consideration of the exodus story in this chapter.)[9]

Ricoeur's primary concern is the defining question of hermeneutics, namely the opposition "between explanation and understanding."[10] This opposition grows out of questions raised by influential German philosophers in the eighteenth and nineteenth centuries, such as Friedrich Schleiermacher and William Dilthey. To *understand* a text, according to Dilthey, is to enter into the author's mind, "to know something of [the author's] mental life through the perceptible signs which manifest it."[11] For Schleiermacher, the point of hermeneutics is to grasp the author's genius; to understand a text is to use it to "understand an author as well as and even better than he understands himself."[12] To *explain* a text, on the other hand, is to identify the rules it follows, following a conception of knowledge modelled after forms of inductive reasoning in the natural sciences, in contrast to the humanist mode of interpretation designated by *understanding*.[13]

These approaches, however, lead to conceptual problems. The first should be clear in light of the discussion of distanciation in the last chapter: to focus on an author's inner psyche, where genius and intention both reside, is to neglect the fact that the author's

---

9 John Durham Peters, *Speaking into the Air: A History of the Idea of Communication*; James Carey, *Communication as Culture: Essays on Media and Society*; Kyle Conway, *Little Mosque on the Prairie and the Paradoxes of Cultural Translation*.

10 Ricoeur, *Hermeneutics and the Human Sciences*, 3.

11 Dilthey, quoted in Ricoeur, *Hermeneutics and the Human Sciences*, 112.

12 Schleiermacher, quoted in Ricoeur, *Hermeneutics and the Human Sciences*, 6. For the original context, see Friedrich D. E. Schleiermacher, "General Hermeneutics," 83.

13 Ricoeur, *Hermeneutics and the Human Sciences*, 171. Ricoeur, like the authors he cites, tends to favour the German verbs *erklären* for "explain" and *verstehen* for "understand."

intention is outside the reader's ken. The author is not available to rein in the polysemy inherent in their words, and readers have only the text itself to interpret. There's no need to rehearse the argument here: it's the point of chapter 1.

The problem with explanation—the approach where we try to arrive inductively at an account of how a text produces meaning—is more subtle. This approach is like solving a jigsaw puzzle. The text is like the cover of the box, and the pieces—the different parts of the text—are inside. The task is to put the pieces together to see how each relates to all the others, until the puzzle looks like the box top, or the pieces fit together to form the text. The problem arises from the fact that explanation in this sense provides an account of how the text functions but not how it relates to the world outside itself.

Here's a concrete example, that of structuralism, from the early- to mid-twentieth century. In the founding work of structural linguistics, the *Cours de linguistique générale* (published in English as the *Course in General Linguistics*), Ferdinand de Saussure divides the phenomena of language into two categories: *langue*, or the structure that produces meaning in language, and *parole*, or the actual instances where people create messages using the tools that this structure provides. (The French words *langue* and *parole* do not have tidy equivalents in English. *Langue* means "language," in the sense of a system of verbal and written signs that can be described by a dictionary and a grammar book, the first providing words and the second the rules to combine them. In that sense, it describes the structural capacity to speak. At the same time, national languages such as English or French are also *langues*. As for *parole*, it means "speech" or acts of communication.)

For Saussure, the proper object of linguistics is *langue*, or the system that makes communication possible, even if it is knowable only through acts of *parole*. Within the system of *langue*, words come to have meaning as a result of their relationship to other words. It's a negative relationship, in that words are defined by what they are *not*. For instance, at the level of the signifier (or the sounds that speakers say or communicate in a written form), an English speaker recognizes *cat* because it's not *bat* or *mat* or *sat*, or *cut* or *cot*, or *cap* or *can*. At the level of the signified (or that to which a signifier refers—essentially, the idea that a word denotes), that same English speaker recognizes a domestic four-legged feline (a cat) because it's not a four-legged feline at the zoo (a lion), nor a domestic four-legged canine (a dog). Different languages—different *langues*—organize signifiers and signifieds in different ways, but following the same negative logic. *Un chat n'est pas un rat ni un chut ni un char.*[14]

Saussure's ideas resonated with a range of thinkers such as literary scholar Roland Barthes, anthropologist Claude Lévi-Strauss, and political theorist Louis Althusser, who applied his ideas to popular culture, social systems, and politics, respectively.[15] In that respect, their work was hermeneutic: they were interpreting wrestling matches and advertisements for spaghetti (Barthes), cultural groups in South America (Lévi-Strauss), and apparatuses of the state (Althusser). The problem, according to Ricoeur, was that the systems they investigated were closed: if words had meaning only in relation to other words, they never left the abstract realm of *langue* for the concrete world inhabited by actual people. The same was true, paradoxically perhaps, for the signifying systems that structuralist thinkers used to explain other objects of study, even when those objects appeared to belong to the concrete world, as in the case of Lévi-Strauss or Althusser. The systems were closed in on themselves.

14 French for "A cat is not a rat nor a shush nor a tank." The point of the example is rather obscured in translation!

15 Roland Barthes, "Myth Today"; Claude Lévi-Strauss, *Tristes Tropiques*; Louis Althusser, "Ideology and Ideological State Apparatuses (Notes Towards an Investigation)."

Guess and Validation

Ricoeur reaches outside of these systems by borrowing from the speech act theory of philosophers of language such as J. L. Austin and John Searle, according to whom

> the act of discourse is constituted by a hierarchy of subordinate acts distributed on three levels: (1) the level of the locutionary or propositional act, the act *of* saying; (2) the level of the illocutionary act (or force), what we do *in* saying; (3) the level of the perlocutionary act, what we do *by the fact that* we speak.[16]

For example, I say, "It's cold" (my locutionary act), but I'm really making a request, "Please close the window" (my statement's illocutionary force), and you understand it as such and close the window (its perlocutionary force). This move allows Ricoeur to reframe the understanding/explanation dichotomy as a dialectic—a relationship of mutual influence between the subjective and objective dimensions of a text. This new frame provides tools to begin to engage in the process of guessing and validation that we will follow as we interpret a text (see figure 5).

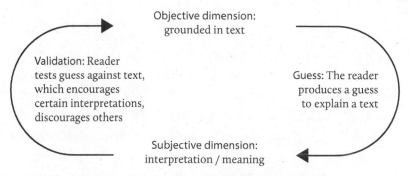

Objective dimension: grounded in text

Validation: Reader tests guess against text, which encourages certain interpretations, discourages others

Guess: The reader produces a guess to explain a text

Subjective dimension: interpretation / meaning

Figure 5. The dialectic relationship between the objective and subjective dimensions of interpretation, mediated through guesses and acts of validation.

---

16 Ricoeur, *Hermeneutics and the Human Sciences*, 96–97, original emphasis. For Austin's account, see *How to Do Things with Words*, lectures 8 and 9.

For Ricoeur, the objective dimension (reflecting concerns addressed by previous thinkers under the rubric of *explanation*) is that of the obdurate, stubborn text, whose fixed content will not admit of fanciful invention. Consider what is surely the most succinct argument about hermeneutics in the history of English-language children's literature, which appears in Lewis Carroll's *Through the Looking-Glass*. The plucky hero Alice, having passed through a mirror in the drawing room of her house, encounters Humpty Dumpty, sitting on a wall. Like everyone else she meets, he's impertinent and speaks in riddles. After making what he thinks is an especially clever point about the merits of "unbirthdays," he proclaims, "There's a glory for you!" Alice says she doesn't understand, and he explains that a glory is a "a nice knock-down argument." Alice objects that a person can't make a word mean whatever they want, to which Humpty Dumpty responds:

> "When *I* use a word . . . it means just what I choose it to mean— neither more nor less."
> "The question is," said Alice, "whether you *can* make words mean so many different things."
> "The question is," said Humpty Dumpty, "which is to be master—that's all."[17]

Ricoeur would side with Alice here. Words might be polysemic, but their meaning is not entirely free-floating. The same is true of texts: they are open to multiple interpretations, but not ones made from whole cloth. If texts did not act as an anchor for interpretation, they could neither make claims nor build worlds.

The subjective dimension (reflecting concerns addressed under the rubric of *understanding*) is that of meaning itself. We make meaning of a text (using strategies I describe below), but that meaning is held in check by the text. By drawing attention to this relationship between meaning and text, Ricoeur overcomes the opposition

---

17 Lewis Carroll, *Through the Looking-Glass*, chap. 6.

between understanding and explanation advanced by his predecessors, who treated them as irreconcilable. He shows that they are in fact linked, each exerting influence over the other.

In this way, hermeneutics becomes an argumentative discipline: a text has no "true" or fixed meaning because its objective dimension—its unchanging content—is inextricably linked to the act of meaning-making. Instead, readers must demonstrate that their interpretation suits the text-as-anchor better than others. In effect, Ricoeur establishes a different warrant (the "standard the researcher applies to assess the merits of the data supporting a claim")[18] for hermeneutics than for the social sciences from which the idea of explanation borrowed. It follows a logic of probability rather than verifiability. In this respect, he hearkens back to Aristotle, who saw the persuasion at the heart of rhetoric in a similar way. For Aristotle, a speaker could convince listeners in one of two ways. The first was through irrefutable evidence: the fact that a person had a fever was a sign that they were sick.[19] The second was through an appeal to what was likely. This approach was more common, for instance in a court case where there were no witnesses, a situation that gave Greek jurists room to argue that "the judges must decide from what is probable; that this is meant by 'giving a verdict in accordance with one's honest opinion'; that probabilities cannot be bribed to mislead the court; and that probabilities are never convicted of perjury."[20] It was only in the second case that persuasion was necessary, as irrefutable facts, according to Aristotle, presented no other possible interpretation.

---

18 Gerianne Merrigan, Carole L. Huston, and Russell Johnston, *Communication Research Methods*, 8.

19 Aristotle, *Rhetoric*, Book 1, Part 2, 1357b. Aristotle uses *sign* here to describe this relationship of necessity. In current usage, *sign* designates a larger class of ideas, but his use is consistent with what Charles Peirce describes as an *index*, or a sign characterized by a relationship of cause and effect, such as smoke, which is an index for fire. Peirce, "Logic as Semiotic: The Theory of Signs."

20 Aristotle, *Rhetoric*, Book 1, Part 15, 1376a.

How do we go about engaging in this process? In order to argue that one interpretation is better than another, we must first propose an interpretation, and for that, we must make a guess, as prosaic as that sounds. Lost and disoriented, we take a stab at it: *Might the author mean _____?* It might feel precarious to take that risk: other people might be smarter, and we might be wrong. (I constantly felt this way when I was a student. My classmates often said things that seemed so brilliant that I couldn't even guess what they meant, let alone what the text we were discussing meant. Later I learned that this feeling is called "imposter syndrome," and everyone experiences it.) But here Ricoeur is reassuring: "there are no rules for making good guesses, but there are methods for validating our guesses."[21] When you're dangling in the void, you reach out for whatever will hold you, and if you grab something solid enough, you start to pull yourself up.

I'm not entirely convinced, however, that there are no rules for making good guesses. Over time, we develop tools for validating guesses, as Ricoeur suggests, and when we start to recognize familiar situations (authors making similar arguments, for instance), we can anticipate the process of validation in order to formulate stronger guesses in the first place. In fact, Ricoeur himself provides two basic strategies for guessing (table 3). We can find clues, and we can relate the parts of a text to the whole (and vice versa). Clues—statements or claims that X is Y or A does B—make certain interpretations likely and others unlikely. Our task is to determine which unsuitable interpretations they exclude or which suitable ones they encourage. The most probable interpretation will prove consistent with the greatest number of facets of the text. This is the logic of probability. Our first goal, despite the mouthful of words in this paragraph, is accuracy, or what Ricoeur describes as congruence. Does our interpretation

---

21 Ricoeur, *Hermeneutics and the Human Sciences*, 137, paraphrasing Eric Hirsch. Note that Karl Popper, working in a very different tradition (that of the natural sciences), makes a similar observation: "There is no such thing," he says, "as a logical method of having new ideas . . . every discovery contains 'an irrational element', or 'a creative intuition'." Popper, *The Logic of Scientific Discovery*, 8.

Table 3. Strategies for guessing and criteria for validation

	Strategies for guessing	Criteria for validation	Goal
Find clues	Determine which suitable interpretations the clues encourage, and which unsuitable interpretations they exclude	The most probable interpretation accounts for the greatest number of facets of the text (logic of probability)	Explain text accurately (congruence)
Relate parts to whole	Ask how different parts of text work together	The parts will be consistent with the whole, and the whole will clarify the parts	Understand text fully (plenitude)

Source: Ricoeur, *Hermeneutics and the Human Sciences,* chapters 6 and 8.

reflect the content of the text? Does the content of the text support our interpretation?[22]

We can also ask how different parts of the text work together. Ricoeur compares texts to three dimensional objects that can be observed from different angles. To describe the entire object—or the entire text—is to see how its parts combine to form a whole: "It is always possible to relate the same sentence in different ways to this or that sentence considered as the cornerstone of the text. A specific kind of onesidedness is implicit in the act of reading. This onesidedness confirms the guess character of interpretation."[23] In accomplishing this task, we achieve a second goal, which Ricoeur describes as plenitude. As we move from congruence to plenitude, we move from technical explanation to interpretation and understanding.

This is the approach I have taken here. Consider my notes (reproduced in figure 6) for table 2, included in the previous chapter. My goal was to take Ricoeur's disparate comments on metaphor, text,

---

22 Ricoeur, *Hermeneutics and the Human Sciences,* 138.

23 Ricoeur, *Hermeneutics and the Human Sciences,* 174.

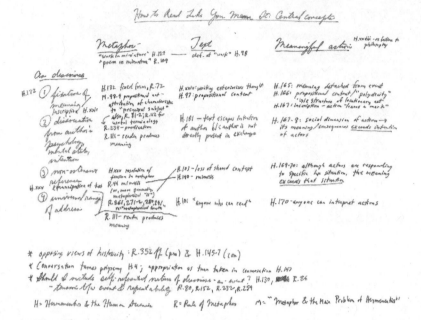

Figure 6. My working notes relating the parts to the whole in Ricoeur's works on metaphor, text, and meaningful action

and meaningful action, spread across a series of lectures and a collection of essays,[24] and to trace the links between them, asking how his treatment of one made it possible to see the others in new ways. If you compare my notes to the figure in its final form, you'll see the working-through process, where I validate and revise my guesses. For instance, my draft version has only four rows (instead of five, as in table 2), and they're in a different order than the one I finally settled upon. In addition, some of my attempts to draw connections are less sure than others. For example, my notes about metaphor's fixed form are especially tentative. To be honest, I made extrapolations that I think are open to critique. My claims are not as persuasive as they'd be if Ricoeur addressed metaphor's fixed form explicitly. (Maybe he

---

24 Ricoeur's *The Rule of Metaphor* consists of a series of lectures he delivered at various universities in North America and Europe, while *Hermeneutics and the Human Sciences* is a collection of articles published over the course of the 1970s.

did, and I just haven't found that book yet. If you sense my nervousness, think about your own. I'm arguing that my reading is plausible, or that someone reading the same things would probably arrive at a similar conclusion. That's your task, too: stake out a claim, even if doing so makes you uneasy.)

The strategy of relating the parts to the whole provides another tool for evaluating claims. One way to see these relationships is as chains of associations (a point I alluded to briefly in chapter 1). As we observe a text from different angles, putting our observations together to see the whole, we're describing chains of associations contained within the text. Consider, for instance, how Ricoeur speaks of probability (figure 7). He refers to Aristotle and to the human sciences. He also refers to the natural sciences and to concepts such as falsifiability, concepts that draw together his entire interpretive schema: "To the procedures of validation also belong procedures of invalidation similar to the criteria of falsifiability emphasised by Karl Popper in his *Logic of Scientific Discovery*. The role of falsification is played here by the conflict between competing interpretations. An interpretation must not only be probable, but more probable than others."[25]

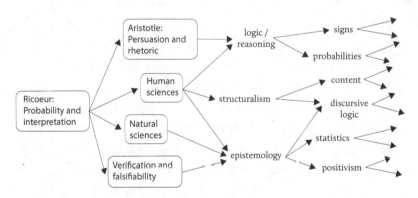

Figure 7. A partial representation of the intertextual associations evoked by Ricoeur in his discussion of probability

---

25 Ricoeur, *Hermeneutics and the Human Sciences*, 175. Mark this point, as we'll come back to it in chapter 4.

Those ideas in turn relate to others: Aristotle applies ideas of probability to logic and reasoning. The human sciences, as they strive for a mode of objectivity modelled after that of the natural sciences, develop paradigms such as structuralism, and, along with the natural sciences, raise questions of epistemology. The discussion of verification and falsifiability raises similar questions. These ideas, in turn, point to still others: signs and probabilities (in Aristotle's technical sense), content, discursive logic, even statistics and the positivism in which they are grounded. And those ideas point to still others.

My sketch here is incomplete. There is no way, in fact, to circumscribe the chain of associations within Ricoeur's texts, if we also investigate the ideas in the texts to which he refers, and in those to which they refer in turn, and so on. But the challenge doesn't stop there. We must deal not just with congruence, but with plenitude, too: "All of the connotations which are suitable," Ricoeur says, "must be attributed."[26] As soon as we reach beyond the limits of the text, the potential connotations are unlimited. Consider my structuralism example: Ricoeur refers to Saussure, and Saussure refers to others (whom Ricoeur doesn't necessarily address), who refer to still others, and so on.

Viewed in this way, the task of interpretation is one of situating a text within the networks of association constituted by those chains. This is an inexhaustible task. In conceptual terms, that's because there are always more texts. In practical terms, that's because there are always more readers. My network likely overlaps with yours to a large degree (a fact that makes communication possible) but not entirely, as we've led different lives. Two people might read the same words in the same order, but because they're reading against different conceptual horizons formed by their respective experiences with the texts in question, they will not arrive at the same interpretation.

For this reason, plenitude is not merely about relating the parts of a text to the whole, and the whole to the parts. It's also about

---

26 Ricoeur, *Hermeneutics and the Human Sciences*, 138, quoting Monroe Beardsley.

relating the parts to the other texts to which the author is responding. This network is the source of the text's plurivocity (or textual polysemy—its multiple, competing meanings). It is also the reason that interpretation follows a logic of probability rather than certainty. One reader can contest another's claim about what a text means by resituating it within a different network of associations.

All of this leads me back to Ricoeur's assertion that "there are no rules for making good guesses." One the one hand, I said I'm not convinced. On the other, the complexity of these networks makes hazarding a guess tricky. To read in a radical sense—to read like you mean it—is to approach a text with no preconceptions, in which case the first guess is in fact a stab in the dark. (If you apply what you think you know about a text, you run the risk of reaching conclusions about it even before you read it.) We will never have all the information we need in order to act, and yet we need to act. And in acting—we guess, we validate, we revise our guess—we come to discover the things we did not know when we started out.

In the sections that follow, I look at examples of people who wandered and how they made their first guesses as they tried to orient themselves. In the next chapters, especially chapter 4, I focus on the process of validation, or how, through guessing, we find the perspective that leads us out of the wilderness.

Floundering in the Time of Pandemic

I opened this chapter by talking about the COVID-19 pandemic. Perhaps you know how this pandemic ends. I do not. That gut-level feeling of uncertainty is what I'm trying to evoke as a way to illustrate the disorientation we feel when we're negated by a text. I'm floundering—and so too, it seems, is the whole world. The world we knew no longer exists: the life we knew has been negated.

The best illustration of this disorientation comes from the months right after different regions went into lockdown. It was the moment where we all felt like the hapless pilot whose flying contraption has just collapsed (the image I discussed in chapter 1). We were all grasping for whatever solid object we could find to support our weight, anything to orient ourselves in a world where our trusted reference points were gone.

To make sense of the pandemic, people made guesses, in Ricoeur's sense, by asking, *Does the pandemic mean* _____? Over time, they were able to evaluate their guesses, but at first, they had to take a stab in the dark. This section focuses on people who made a professional habit of interpreting events, such as teachers, artists, and religious leaders, who had all cultivated their hermeneutic skills but, as we'll see, still felt ill-equipped to deal with the transformations the world was undergoing. It goes without saying that my sample is not representative. Instead, the value of these people's interventions came from their public nature and from the fact that the authors were people to whom others turned for guidance.

As I wrote in the introduction, the pandemic constituted a meaningful action in Ricoeur's sense of the term. Consider the five qualities that characterize metaphors, texts, and meaningful actions (table 2 in chapter 1): their propositional claims, their fixed content, the unknowable intent of their authors, their potentially limitless audience, and their non-ostensive worlds. Of those, four are easy to identify with respect to the pandemic:

- *The content is fixed*: The pandemic has "left its mark," so to speak, as it has changed how we interact with the world.
- *The author's intention is distant*: The many actors in the pandemic—public health professionals, governmental leaders, other members of the public, the virus itself—are not present to explain their actions to us.
- *The audience is potentially limitless*: The pandemic affects everyone, and everyone interprets it.
- *The world referred to is not that of the immediate environment*: When people interpret the pandemic, they do so in different contexts.

The remaining quality—the idea that people attribute meaning to an action—is simultaneously the most difficult and the most important for understanding how they approached the pandemic.

It was clear, on the one hand, that people felt driven to interpret what was happening. "We are not well designed, it seems, to live in uncertainty," according to humanities professor Mark Lilla.[27] The problem, on the other hand, was that there was little if any meaning to be found. Doctors and nurses treating COVID patients found themselves at a loss even to express their own grief.[28] Writer Leslie Jamison compared the social loss of the pandemic to the personal loss she experienced at the same time—a divorce, first, but also the loss of the senses of taste and smell, a symptom that doctors would link to COVID soon after she contracted the disease. For her, the pandemic was marked by "a certain cognitive dissonance" in the encounter of "something as surreal and unfamiliar as a global pandemic from inside the deadening familiarity and cloistered banality of our apartment—an extraordinary event experienced from inside a parade of days textured by unceasing ordinariness, the daily loop of domesticity."[29]

Jamison made sense of the loss through a metaphor, *the social experience of the pandemic is like the personal experience of loss*, but the incommensurable tension between the objects she was comparing, the social and personal dimensions of experience, complicated rather than simplified her understanding of what was happening around her:

> Sometimes loss just feels like loss, and absence is just absence:
> the solipsism of pain; the ache of losing touch; the empty
> streets and bankruptcies, the missing ventilators, the bodies
> stored in the temporary morgues of moving vans. The trick
> is how to hold both truths at once—absence-as-presence and

---

27 Mark Lilla, "No One Knows What's Going to Happen."
28 Ron Suskind, "Doctors Are Covid's First Historians."
29 Leslie Jamison, "When the World Went Away, We Made a New One."

absence-as-absence—rather than letting one obscure the other; how to let fragile, unexpected, imperfect consolations exist alongside everything they can't console.[30]

Rodrigo García went a step further in a letter to his father, the late Colombian novelist Gabriel García Márquez. For him, the pandemic represented not just loss without meaning, but loss without even the chance to redeem it as meaningful: "It's not just death that frightens us, but the circumstances. A final exit without goodbyes, attended by strangers dressed as extraterrestrials, machines beeping heartlessly, surrounded by others in similar situations, but far from our people."[31]

Faced with this void, what do people do? Some reject the demand that we find meaning that does not exist: "A dose of humility," Lilla suggests, "would do us good in the present moment. It might also help reconcile us to the radical uncertainty in which we are always living."[32] Others make guesses, asking, *Does the pandemic teach us the same thing as* _____? (figure 8). Like Jamison, they use metaphor, a form of meaningful discourse on a smaller scale, to identify the propositional claims (concerned, for example, with the new relationships we are forming with others) that they might attribute to the pandemic. What can we learn from people with similar experiences (the loss of one's house, or cancer, or a midlife career change)?

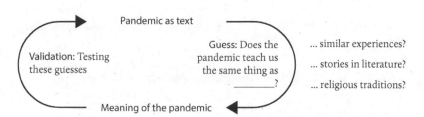

Figure 8. Interpreting the pandemic through the process of guessing and validation

---

30 Jamison, "When the World Went Away, We Made a New One."

31 Rodrigo García, "A Letter to My Father, Gabriel García Márquez."

32 Lilla, "No One Knows What's Going to Happen."

After the first few months, as new routines began to set in, journalists began compiling "rule book"-type lists of what to do in the face of uncertainty: "First, reflect on how you're feeling and on what's still good. . . . [Second,] try to set aside other people's expectations."[33] Or, more practically,

1. Check the health of your state and community
2. Limit the number of your close contacts
3. Manage your exposure budget
4. Keep higher risk activities as short as possible
5. Keep taking pandemic precautions[34]

But these lists were as much about the day-to-day challenges of manoeuvring through difficult times as they were about what those difficulties meant. Venturing further afield, what insight might literature provide? The turn to literature shouldn't be surprising. As Jonathan Culler explains, "experience is always mediated by signs and the 'original'" and the experience we have that we think is somehow new "is produced as an effect of signs, of supplements."[35] In other words, we interpret our experience through stories we've read or heard or seen about others. (If you've ever taken an online quiz to know which character from your favourite show you "are," you've experienced this mediation. One appeal of stories is the way that we come to understand ourselves better through the actions of others.) García notes in his letter to his father, "Not a day goes by that I don't come across a reference to your novel 'Love in the Time of Cholera,' or a riff on its title or to the insomnia pandemic in 'One Hundred Years of Solitude.'"[36]

These approaches are all guesses, and they call for validation. Do they represent our experience accurately (congruence, as in

33 National Public Radio, "Advice for Dealing with Uncertainty, From People Who've Been There."
34 Tara Parker-Pope, "5 Rules to Live By During a Pandemic."
35 Jonathan Culler, *Literary Theory: A Very Short Introduction*, 12.
36 García, "A Letter to My Father, Gabriel García Márquez."

table 3 above)? Do they help us see new dimensions of our experience (plenitude)? If they reveal new dimensions, do those new insights in turn lead us to make new guesses? And how, then, do those guesses represent our experience in all its dimensions? To see this process in greater detail, I want to turn to one metaphor that was frequently evoked in the first few months of the pandemic. It is the metaphor of the Israelites wandering for forty years in the desert, in the books of Exodus and Numbers, versions of which are found in all Abrahamic religions, primary among them Judaism, Christianity, and Islam. Although people evoked other stories, such as that of Job or of disciples setting out on the road,[37] the story of the Israelites in the desert resonated more widely and provides a valuable example of the iterative cycle of guess and validation.[38]

Wandering in the Desert

Exodus and Numbers are the second and fourth books of Moses.[39] Exodus tells the story of how Moses was born and how God called him to free the Israelites, who were slaves in Egypt. Numbers tells the story of the forty years the Israelites spent wandering in the desert, waiting to arrive in the land of Canaan, which God had promised them when they left Egypt. These are the stories that make Moses a central figure in the Abrahamic religions. They are also the stories that hold especial meaning for oppressed people and others who feel they are wandering: "many racial-ethnic and women's

---

37 Lilla, "No One Knows What's Going to Happen"; Emily M. D. Scott, "Start Looking, and You'll See Roads All Over the Bible."

38 For example, Mariann Edgar Budde, "Wandering the COVID-19 Wilderness"; Rukhl Schaechter, "It's 2020 and We're Wandering in the Desert Once Again."

39 For an overview, see Katharine Doob Sakenfeld, "Numbers," and Nyasha Junior, "Exodus." I am indebted in this section to Rev. Erin Burns, the chaplain at Queen's University in Kingston, Ontario, for our conversations that helped me think through the metaphor of wandering in the desert.

groups, believing that God has promised a better future, have constructively appropriated the biblical theme of a wilderness journey."[40] Hence their appeal in the COVID era, too.

That these books are imbued with meaning should come as no surprise. The word *sign* appears thirty times in Exodus—the book is swimming in signs.[41] God convinces Moses to be his messenger (along with his brother Aaron; they are later joined by their sister Miriam) with a sign, turning his rod into a snake and then back into a rod. God tells the Israelites to put the blood of a lamb on their doorposts as a sign not to kill their firstborn sons, an event still marked each year in the observation of Passover.

Numbers, as its name implies, is a book about counting, full of censuses and measurements, as the Israelites count how many people there are in each of the twelve tribes (descended from the twelve sons of Jacob) and follow God's instructions about how to conduct their rituals of worship and purification. Where Exodus is full of forward movement, as Moses leads the Israelites out of Egypt, Numbers is full of waiting, with many Israelites coming to doubt that leaving Egypt was the right idea at all.

The life the Israelites led in Egypt was difficult. When Moses first approaches Pharaoh, he conveys a message from God: "Thus says the LORD, the God of Israel, 'Let my people go, that they may hold a feast to me in the wilderness.'"[42] Not only does Pharaoh refuse, saying that he does not recognize this god, but he decides that the request is a sign that the Israelites do not have enough work. He instructs his taskmasters to stop supplying them with the straw they need to make bricks, forcing them to find their own. The taskmasters beat them when they cannot make as many bricks as before. When Moses demands again that Pharaoh release the Israelites, Pharaoh refuses again, and Moses tells the Pharaoh that God will visit

---

40 Sakenfeld, "Numbers," 81.

41 I am using the Revised Standard Version of the Bible.

42 Exodus 5:1.

plagues upon the Egyptians "that [they] may know that there is no one like the LORD our God."[43] God sends frogs, locusts, and pestilence, until finally, for the tenth and final plague, God kills all of the Egyptians' firstborn sons and firstborn cattle. Even when Pharaoh releases the Israelites, his army pursues them toward the Red Sea. When the Israelites reach its shore, Moses lifts his rod, and the sea parts. The Israelites pass through it, but when the Egyptians enter it, "The waters returned and covered the chariots and the horsemen and all the host of Pharaoh that had followed them into the sea; not so much as one of them remained."[44] Then the Israelites enter the wilderness.

Two aspects of their lives in the wilderness are especially useful for understanding how their story helped people understand their lives during the COVID-19 pandemic. On the one hand, the Israelites start to establish a new routine. Six days a week, God sends them manna, which "was like coriander seed, white, and the taste of it was like wafers made with honey,"[45] with instructions that they gather enough for the day or for two days, if the following day is a one of rest. They also establish new laws, most famously the Ten Commandments, but also rules about how to offer sacrifices, conduct rituals, and keep themselves ritually clean. They even begin to organize what looks to contemporary eyes like a bureaucratic structure for administering justice, when Jethro, Moses' father-in-law, advises Moses to appoint capable individuals "as rulers of thousands, of hundreds, of fifties, and of tens."[46] These are tools they need for their large community, which includes more than 600,000 men who are able to fight, according to the census taken at the beginning of Numbers.[47]

---

43 Exodus 8:10.

44 Exodus 14:28.

45 Exodus 16:31.

46 Exodus 18:21.

47 Numbers 1:46. The census includes only these men, suggesting that the community was much larger.

On the other hand, the Israelites are restless. They have been uprooted from everything they knew, to which they harbour a strange desire to return. Without their old points of reference, they complain repeatedly to Moses, saying: "Would that we had died by the hand of the LORD in the land of Egypt, when we sat by the fleshpots and ate bread to the full; for you have brought us out into this wilderness to kill this whole assembly with hunger."[48] In their drive to understand what has become of their lives, they turn toward the familiar, even if what was familiar was slavery. Eventually, their complaints will prove so frustrating that God will threaten to "strike them with pestilence and disinherit them."[49] Moses intercedes on their behalf, and God relents, but not without punishing them, saying, "Your children shall be shepherds in the wilderness forty years, and shall suffer for your faithlessness, until the last of your dead bodies lies in the wilderness . . . you shall bear your iniquity, forty years, and you shall know my displeasure."[50]

Thus there are two generations of Israelites in these stories, the first that leaves Egypt with Moses, the second that is born in the wilderness. The difference between the two, according to Katharine Sakenfeld, is that the second generation is more obedient.[51] Another way to interpret the difference is to recognize that the second generation does not have first-hand experience of life in Egypt: all they know is the wilderness, which provides the points of reference the first generation lacked. The routine that began to develop in the early years of wandering has continued to settle in, so that the wilderness no longer feels so disorienting. Thus there are fewer "murmurings against the LORD," which is to say, fewer complaints.[52]

48 Exodus 16:3. See also Exodus 14:11–12 and Numbers 11:4–6, 14:2–3, 16:13, 20:3–5, and 21:5.

49 Numbers 14:12.

50 Numbers 14:33–34.

51 Sakenfeld, "Numbers," 79–80.

52 Exodus 16:7.

When the sons of two families ask permission to build a settlement just outside the land of Canaan for their families, where they can graze their sheep, Moses warns them that God will be angry if they settle down and do not take up arms as the other men must do. They respond, "As the LORD has said to your servants, so we will do," an answer God finds more pleasing than the complaints from the prior generation.[53]

Here we return to Ricoeur as a way to see how the stories of Exodus and Numbers serve as interpretive lenses for people during the COVID-19 pandemic. As with the pandemic, we can see how wandering in the wilderness was a meaningful action for the Israelites. Its content was fixed, in that wandering "left its mark," changing how the Israelites interacted with the world. The author's intention was distant: the Israelites could not know God's mind. The audience was limitless: the Israelites interpreted wandering as they experienced it (not to mention the fact that members of the Abrahamic religions have continued to interpret it in new ways). And those varied audiences have interpreted the wandering in a variety of contexts. That of the first generation was not that of the second, just as the context in which people interpret the events now is not that of the Israelites' lived experience.

What remains is the question of meaning itself. Here again we see the process of guessing and validation. The complaints from members of the first generation who said they had been led out of Egypt only to meet a new type of hardship suggest that they thought that wandering meant that God had forsaken them. But the view of the second generation is perhaps more interesting, as it shows how meaning evolves as people's situation evolves. As Sakenfeld points out, the book of Numbers describes a second census, which yields a very similar count.[54] The purpose of this count is to give each family a parcel of land proportionate to its size, but the fact that the count

53 Numbers 32:31.

54 Numbers 26:51.

remains the same is a sign suggesting "divine faithfulness despite the pattern of persistent rebellion."[55] Hence a second interpretation of the action of wandering: rather than meaning that God has forsaken the Israelites, it appears to mean that God has protected them.

Conclusion: From the "Literal *Is Not*" to the "Metaphorical *Is*"

My analysis here is nested. People seeking to explain the COVID-19 pandemic evoked the story of the Israelites in the desert, which is also about seeking to explain experiences of disorientation. What lessons can contemporary commentators draw from the Israelites? Perhaps the most salient is that routine develops even in new situations, and it provides the context for people to reorient themselves. That has certainly been the case for me. A funny thing happened after I started this chapter: time passed, and the world began to open up again. As I write, the province where I live now allows people to move around a bit more: restaurants are open, as are parks and public areas, but everyone must wear a mask. We haven't returned to the way things were, but I've seen more of the world outside of my basement than I had when I wrote this chapter's introduction. My family has found a new routine and new points of reference. There is still uncertainty, such as how schools will operate when my children return to them in a month, but I feel oriented again, better equipped to make choices (such as about instructional modalities for my kids) that require me to interpret the world in which we now live.

In effect, what I am experiencing is a passage from the "literal *is not*" to the "metaphorical *is*," to return to a distinction from the introductory chapter—from the negation of chapter 1 and consequent wandering of chapter 2 to an exploration of the new space opened up by metaphors, texts, and meaningful actions, which are the focus of chapters 3 and 4. As with my other examples, we can

---

55 Sakenfeld, "Numbers," 81.

see this transition by looking at people's lived experience of the pandemic. As different regions have come out of confinement, people have acted on their pent-up energy. Many experienced relief; others something closer to euphoria. That euphoria is the subject of the next chapter.

3

To Read Is to Feel Love

You will not be surprised to learn that some books are so exciting that they keep me up at night. I read them to enter a new world, one that opens up before me like a flower unfolding in the morning sun.

The most recent book to have this effect on me was Shawn Wilson's *Research Is Ceremony: Indigenous Research Methods*. It asks questions similar to those I'm asking in this book, questions that, for me, seem to move under their own power or volition. How do people talk across cultural borders? How do they cultivate a shared vocabulary to counter the social and political forces that work against mutual understanding? How do they cultivate something like empathy? Wilson even asks one of the questions I meditate on in this book: how do we writers establish a relationship with our readers, who could be anybody? What I find exciting is that his answers are so different from my own. He writes his book to his children, prefacing the early chapters with letters addressed to them. He uses these letters to draw in interlopers like me. It is a gesture of generosity and discovery to me, at once simple and effective, but also an approach that I, coming from a cultural background where we attend to relationships in a different way, would never have arrived at on my own.

And yet there's a point that really sticks for me. He recounts a story told to him by a friend and colleague, Cora Weber-Pillwax. She happens upon a scholarly article by an anthropologist who she realizes is writing about her community. She finds the anthropologist "arrogant and aggressive" because he misinterprets what he sees and, in his carelessness, he throws the relationships Weber-Pillwax values out of balance.[1] I will give only these general contours to her story because I run the same risk of carelessness as the anthropologist and I want to respect the precepts Weber-Pillwax and Wilson set out for ethical engagement with Indigenous communities, including relational accountability.[2] These are also the only details necessary to understand my reaction to this passage, a reaction that surprised me. Because the anthropologist and I likely share a similar background, I interpreted his actions differently. I didn't see arrogance and aggression but cluelessness in good faith. I had to ask myself, why was I sticking up for someone whose work clearly caused harm to the community he was studying? Part of the answer, I think, is that I have seen this pattern of interactions before, where people who do not share my background interpret my actions through their own cultural lens, missing my meaning without even realizing they've missed it. I admit it makes me defensive. Was that what was happening here? But I'm also self-aware enough to know that I am prone to misinterpreting people unlike me, too. I felt conflicted: on the one hand, Wilson's book was one of the most exciting things I had read in a long time because it addressed urgent questions in ways that were new to me, but on the other, I had a gut reaction to a passage that I could not have predicted. I'll return to this reaction in the conclusion, where it will make more sense in light of the rest of the chapter. (At

---

1 Cora Weber-Pillwax, quoted in Shawn Wilson, *Research Is Ceremony: Indigenous Research Methods*, 72.

2 Wilson, *Research Is Ceremony*, 77. I do, however, encourage my readers to read Wilson's book, especially the chapter in which he tells this story. Rarely have I had the pleasure of reading a book so clearly necessary and challenging to my own perspective as a researcher.

the risk of giving away the ending, I have come to agree with Wilson and his friend.)

This chapter is about the conflict between an excitement so strong that readers keep thinking about a book long after they put it down and a visceral reaction where they have to process the idea that what they thought they knew about the world is incomplete or wrong. It addresses themes similar to those in chapter 1, except in a positive valence. The euphoria of reading can be disorienting in the same way as floundering: both involve an element of exhilarating terror. Both risk overrunning their own limits.

This chapter proceeds, first, by asking about texts themselves: what do metaphors—Ricoeur's texts in miniature—show us about how reading can lead to euphoria? Then, to understand the nature of this experience, it takes a detour through ideas of love as they shape how people relate to others. The first account comes from Plato's *Phaedrus*, a dialogue in which Socrates, the main speaker, famously compares the experience of a soul in love to that of a charioteer travelling between heaven and earth, with one steed that obeys him and one that follows its own whims. The second comes from Sappho, who wrote poetry about love two centuries before Plato. Both she and Plato describe love's physical effects on the lover—the faintness, the prickly skin, the stomach tied in knots. The third account is more recent. It comes from the Belgian philosopher Luce Irigaray, who asks whether it is possible to love without turning the person one loves into an object (something of which Plato's Socrates is guilty). Finally, the chapter returns to texts and reading to ask what these accounts of love and its objects reveal about how we open ourselves to the meaning a text can make.

Euphoric Texts

This book's introductory chapter ends with the question that is Paul Ricoeur's starting point where the analysis of metaphor (and, by extension, text and meaningful action) is concerned. What do you do when you both mean what you say, and you don't? In effect, that contradiction is the defining feature of metaphor, whose literal meaning (the comparison of dissimilar things) cannot be true, but whose figurative meaning (to be found in the tension between those things) *is* true, at least when metaphor is effective.

To begin to answer this question, Ricoeur turns to Aristotle. Ricoeur's focus is Aristotle's *Poetics*, a work that exists now only in incomplete form, which describes how the ancient Greek genre of tragedy has an effect on audiences. Tragedy, Aristotle says, is characterized by its unity of plot: it tells one story, and one story only. Its characters are nobler than the members of the audience, and they undergo a reversal of fortune that provokes a catharsis (or emotional release) for the audience. (The end of the *Poetics* hints at an analysis of comedy, but it is lost to history.)

Ricoeur's interest in Aristotle lies, first, in Aristotle's argument that tragedy, comedy, and various forms of poetry and music "are all in their general conception modes of imitation."[3] But later Aristotle also seems to say that tragedy is *more than* imitation. For this reason, according to Aristotle, it's a nobler form than epic poetry, for instance. It has everything epic poetry has, plus things it doesn't, such as music. Its effect on audiences is greater because it can be performed, rather than merely read. Its plot is tighter, and it tells its story more efficiently, heightening the effect on audiences. Thus, because it "fulfills its specific function better as an art—for each art ought to produce, not any chance pleasure, but the pleasure proper to it . . .—it plainly follows that tragedy is the higher art, as attaining its end more perfectly."[4] This conclusion leads Ricoeur to ask, by Aristotle's logic, whether tragedy imitates life, or whether it goes beyond imitation to something more real than real. And this question returns him to metaphor: tragedy and metaphor both

---

3 Aristotle, *Poetics*, Section 1, Part 1, 1447a.

4 Aristotle, *Poetics*, Section 3, Part 26, 1462b.

work by simultaneously imitating the world (or making statements about it) and elevating it. Tragedy elevates the meaning of the life it depicts; metaphor elevates the meaning of the things it compares.[5] In this way, metaphor suggests a new way to relate to the world—or worlds—through which we navigate: "It could be that the everyday reference to the real must be abolished in order that another sort of reference to other dimensions of reality might be liberated."[6] Or, going still further, we must reformulate our understanding of language "such that imagination becomes itself a properly semantic moment of the metaphorical statement."[7]

In other words, for Ricoeur, metaphor attains toward something like myth. Myths tell people about their origins and give them a structure for explaining their experiences. In that respect, they come to define fundamental, even existential truths, even if the people who hear them don't think they're true in a literal sense. Few people today believe that Hermes, the messenger god from Greek mythology, was an actual, embodied deity who flew around on winged sandals, but the ideas he was meant to embody—in particular, the ability to communicate between different realms—are still so meaningful that the field of philosophy we're investigating here, hermeneutics, bears his name.

In Ricoeur's words, "metaphor is that strategy of discourse by which language divests itself of its function of direct description in order to reach the mythic level where its function of discovery is set free."[8] This freedom is the source of the euphoria we feel when we read a particularly compelling book. It demonstrates "the ecstatic moment of language—language going beyond itself."[9] (The word *ecstatic* comes from the Greek ἔκστασις or *ékstasis*, which combines

---

5 Paul Ricoeur, *The Rule of Metaphor: The Creation of Meaning in Language*, 45–46.

6 Ricoeur, *Rule of Metaphor*, 70.

7 Ricoeur, *Rule of Metaphor*, 229.

8 Ricoeur, *Rule of Metaphor*, 292.

9 Ricoeur, *Rule of Metaphor*, 294.

ἔκ or *ek*, meaning "out of," from which we get the prefix *ex-* in English, and στασις or *stasis*, from the word meaning "to stand": literally, to stand outside of oneself.) It's a feeling almost of compulsion, where we strain against the limits of our understanding of the world. It's what leads us in our excitement to embrace—naively, by Ricoeur's account—the world opened up by metaphor at the expense of the challenge posed by metaphor's impossible literal meaning. To give a concrete example, think of anyone who discovers a book that seems to them to have all the answers, and think of their enthusiasm to convert you to their point of view. They are caught up in what I referred to in the introductory chapter (borrowing from Ricoeur) as the "ontological vehemence of the metaphorical 'is.'" (*Ontology* is the philosophy of being and answers the question, "What is _____?" Ricoeur refers to the world that metaphor opens up as the "metaphorical 'is.'" I will return to the idea of ontological vehemence in the concluding chapter.)

To explain through another image Ricoeur uses, that of a plant that itself also becomes a metaphor, this impulse "reaches towards the light and into the earth and draws its growth from them" (figure 9).[10] Gardeners living in Canada (or any other cold place) will understand this. On dark winter days, as daylight begins to creep back into our lives, we dream of tomatoes and basil and Swiss chard. We hoard seeds, which we plant and tend with great care, starting them at just the right time, hardening them off when the days are warm enough, planting them in the ground, fighting off the wretched squirrels that chew them down to nubs when we're not looking. The plants seem to yearn for the sun as we do, thrust forward by a primal, unstoppable force. They burst out of the ground, reaching up, stretching. "So too," writes Ricoeur, "the poetic verb enjoins us to participate in the totality of things via an 'open communion.'"[11]

---

10 Ricoeur, *Rule of Metaphor*, 294–95, paraphrasing Samuel Taylor Coleridge.

11 Ricoeur, *Rule of Metaphor*, 295.

Figure 9. The vital force of eros, like a plant reaching up toward the sun. Source: Philip Reinagle, *American Bog Plants* (1807). OldBookIllustrations.com.

The feeling is one of vertiginous euphoria, or ecstasy in Ricoeur's term. It drives our desire to make sense of the world, to find meaning in its random flux. Another example: one day when my daughter was learning to read, she said that suddenly she saw words everywhere. Where there were letters, there were words, something I took so much for granted that her insight surprised me. Dad, she said, once you learn to read, can you ever *stop*? She understood, in a way she could not yet express, the impulse we have to look for meaning.

With rare exceptions, we want what we do to mean something and not nothing. Even the Old Testament's Ecclesiast, who declares that all is vanity,[12] still looks for meaning in the world. Samuel Rocha, whose work I discuss at the end of this chapter, describes this impulse as eros, or "the virus of fecund desire, the desire for desire," which "begins with the simple fact that we desire to be something: *something instead of nothing.*"[13] It's a desire to find new worlds in what we read: "the properly *epistemological* concerns of hermeneutics," according to Ricoeur, must be "subordinated to *ontological* preoccupations, whereby *understanding* ceases to appear as a simple *mode of knowing* in order to become a *way of being* and a way of relating to beings and being."[14]

Plato, Sappho, and the Struggle of Eros

These are heady ideas, and I tend to get carried away with my multisyllabic words. Would you believe that these ideas put me in the euphoric state I'm describing? I hope that some of my readers might feel the same way. I often teach undergraduate classes of seventy-five or eighty students, and each semester a handful get as excited about these ideas as I do. Others get excited about other things, which is great. What matters is the excitement, not what triggers it.

Here is where a different order of examples is useful. I want to consider two texts, Plato's *Phaedrus* and Sappho's poem known as Fragment 31, which both depict eros—this self-propelled desire— a bit more literally, as expressed in love. In both cases, I'm interested in the relationship they imagine between the lover and the

---

12 Ecclesiastes 1:2.

13 Samuel D. Rocha, *Folk Phenomenology: Education, Study, and the Human Person*, 18.

14 Paul Ricoeur, *Hermeneutics and the Human Sciences: Essays on Language, Action and Interpretation*, 4, original emphasis; cf. Rocha, *Folk Phenomenology*, 16.

beloved and the physical ways people experience the anxiety and excitement of desire.[15]

In the *Phaedrus*, Plato depicts a dialogue between his teacher Socrates and a young man named Phaedrus, who has just heard a speech by Lysias and is eager to discuss it. Phaedrus meets Socrates on the road and is beside himself with excitement. Socrates asks him to repeat the speech, a copy of which Phaedrus is hiding under his cloak. The two find the shade of a tree by a brook and sit down. Phaedrus delivers the speech, according to which a person faced with the choice between someone who loves him (the characters in this dialogue are all men) and someone who doesn't, should choose the person who doesn't because he will be less fickle, less jealous, and will have a confidence that a lover would lack. When he finishes, Phaedrus can't wait to hear Socrates' opinion. But Socrates politely demurs, saying he might have heard better speeches "from Sappho the fair, or Anacreon the wise."[16] Phaedrus beseeches him to give a speech himself, and Socrates obliges by giving two.

The first takes the same line of argument as Lysias (and Phaedrus) but appears to improve upon it. (At the end of the speech, Socrates declares that it was merely a parody.) Socrates warns that

> the irrational desire which overcomes the tendency of opinion towards right, and is led away to the enjoyment of beauty, and especially of personal beauty, by the desires which are her own kindred—that supreme desire, I say, which by leading conquers and by the force of passion is reinforced, from this very force, receiving a name, is called love.[17]

The lover should be spurned in favour of the non-lover because love leads people away from what is right to what is pleasurable. It is

---

15 The word *erotic* derives from *eros*, and as Plato and Sappho show, sexual desire is an exemplary form of erotic drive. But I want to emphasize that it serves here only as one example among others, however. Eros need not be sexual.

16 Plato, *Phaedrus*, 235c.

17 Plato, *Phaedrus*, 238b–c.

worth noting that the translator leaves a note to say the word he has translated as *love* is ἔρως or *eros*, which is also the name of the Greek god of love (better known by his Latin name Cupid), son of Aphrodite (goddess of love) and Ares (god of war).

The theme of eros pervades Socrates' second speech, which he begins after recanting the impiety expressed in his first speech. (He does not want to offend the gods.) He declares that he will speak of the soul, for it is the soul that is at stake in questions of love. Souls themselves are immortal, he says, but people are not. Thus people, who possess souls, are pulled between earthly and heavenly concerns—between corporeal desires and the wisdom that comes from the contemplation of beauty.[18] Plato's Socrates explores this struggle through the image of the charioteer, one of the most famous metaphors in all of Plato's dialogues. The charioteer guides two steeds, the three together representing the soul. The steed on the right is noble in form, "a lover of honour and modesty and temperance, and the follower of true glory," while the one on the left is "a crooked lumbering animal . . . the mate of insolence and pride."[19] The noble horse pulls up, while the bad horse pulls down, and when the charioteer is tempted by love, he and the good steed must fight the bad:

> Now when the charioteer beholds the vision of love, and has his whole soul warmed through sense, and is full of the prickings and ticklings of desire, the obedient steed, then as always under the government of shame, refrains from leaping on the beloved; but the other, heedless of the pricks and of the blows of the

18 In their struggle, the souls of mortals descend from the heavens to the earth, where people belong to one of nine categories, depending on their search for beauty and truth. The most privileged class is that of philosophers, and the least, those of sophists, demagogues, and tyrants. If nothing else, Socrates is looking out for himself! Plato, *Phaedrus*, 248c–e.

19 Plato, *Phaedrus*, 253d–e. The translator notes the significance of the structure of this allegory: "for the first time perhaps in the history of philosophy, we have represented to us the threefold division of psychology," reproduced later, for instance, in the work of Sigmund Freud. Benjamin Jowett, *The Dialogues of Plato*, 410.

whip, plunges and runs away, giving all manner of trouble to his companion and the charioteer, whom he forces to approach the beloved and to remember the joys of love.[20]

The description Socrates gives of the physical sensations of eros—the "prickings and ticklings of desire"—soon turns to terror, as the charioteer and the noble steed fight the bad. It is a violent fight, as the bad steed pulls again and again against the other two, until finally, he

> takes the bit in his teeth and pulls shamelessly. Then the chariot-eer is worse off than ever; he falls back like a racer at the barrier, and with a still more violent wrench drags the bit out of the teeth of the wild steed and covers his abusive tongue and jaws with blood, and forces his legs and haunches to the ground and punishes him sorely.[21]

Only then is he subdued. Still, when the lover finally meets his beloved, "the wanton steed"—that is, the soul's base, physical desire—"has a word to say to the charioteer; he would like to have a little pleasure in return for many pains."[22] He is not so easily tamed after all.

There's an important problem with this account of eros, however. In both speeches, Socrates approaches the beloved as an object. In the parody of Lysias, the beloved is to be dominated; the lover "desires above all things to deprive his beloved of his dearest and best and holiest possessions, father, mother, kindred, friends, of all whom he thinks may be hinderers or reprovers of their most sweet converse."[23] In the speech about the charioteer, the fate of the beloved is

---

20 Plato, *Phaedrus*, 253e–254a. Earlier (251b–c), Socrates describes these physical sensations as the feeling of being "in a state of ebullition and effervescence . . . which may be compared to the irritation and uneasiness in the gums at the time of cutting teeth."

21 Plato, *Phaedrus*, 254d–e.

22 Plato, *Phaedrus*, 255e.

23 Plato, *Phaedrus*, 239e–240a.

not so dramatic, but he remains an "object of [the lover's] worship" nonetheless.[24] The lover fills him with love, and thus the beloved "loves, but he knows not what; he does not understand and cannot explain his own state; he appears to have caught the infection of blindness from another; the lover is his mirror in whom he is beholding himself, but he is not aware of this."[25] The choice to love is out of the hands of the beloved (although, to be fair, the struggle between the charioteer and the bad steed suggests that it's difficult even for the lover to control). As the next section shows, treating the beloved as an object draws the very nature of the relationship defined by love in this sense into question.

In that respect, the poet Sappho provides a useful counter-example. She was born in the seventh century BCE on the Greek island of Lesbos, and she wrote lyric poetry (to be set to music played on the lyre) that was greatly admired in the ancient Greek world. In the *Phaedrus*, as noted above, Socrates mentions her when telling Phaedrus he might have heard speeches better than that of Lysias. However, much of her poetry was lost during Europe's Middle Ages, to the point where she is known now as much by reputation as by the tantalizing fragments of her poetry that remain. With respect to the question of love, although her sexual orientation has been a matter of historical and academic dispute, her poems are sensual and often about women, making her "a feminist heroine or a gay role model, or both."[26]

One of Sappho's best known poems is known as Fragment 31. It describes physical sensations and the mental torment of desire similar to what we find in the *Phaedrus*, but it configures the relation between the lover and her beloved differently. The narrator sees the woman she loves, but she is talking to a man, and the narrator

---

24 Plato, *Phaedrus*, 252a.

25 Plato, *Phaedrus*, 255d.

26 Daniel Mendelsohn, "Girl, Interrupted: Who was Sappho?"; see also Jonathan Goldberg, *Sappho:]fragments*.

is jealous (figure 10). Her relationship to the object of her desire is thus mediated through her envy of the man to whom her beloved is speaking:

> Blest as the immortal gods is he,
> The youth whose eyes may look on thee,
> Whose ears thy tongue's sweet melody
>   May still devour.
> Thou smilest too!—sweet smile, whose charm
> Has struck my soul with wild alarm,
> And, when I see thee, bids disarm
>   Each vital power.
> Speechless I gaze: the flame within

Figure 10. Sappho's narrator spies the woman she loves, whom she cannot approach, and is jealous of the man to whom she is speaking. Sources: Modified from Georges du Maurier, *Vae Victus* (1866) and Harrison Fitcher, *Not Free at All* (1904). OldBookIllustrations.com.

Runs swift o'er all my quivering skin:
My eyeballs swim; with dizzy din
  My brain reels round;
And cold drops fall; and tremblings frail
Seize every limb; and grassy pale
I grow; and then—together fail
  Both sight and sound.[27]

The poem's narrator is consumed by eros—the desire that wells up in her, outside her control—as her skin turns pale and feels like it's burning. She feels dizzy and trembles, but she cannot act directly on her desire. That is the key difference between Sappho's account and that of the *Phaedrus*, and the indirectness of the narrator's approach will help us understand not only the nature of love with (or potentially without) an object, but also ways to approach the texts that give us a feeling of euphoria so that we remain open to what they have to say.

Love Without an Object

How does the beloved in the *Phaedrus* feel about being the object of his lover's desire? That's a trick question. The beloved doesn't get to feel anything: the beloved is an object, not a subject. (Even Sappho's beloved does not escape this condition: she says nothing in Fragment 31, although the poem's narrator cannot act directly upon her.) This fact poses a problem for the charioteer in the *Phaedrus*—and two problems for us. What if we assume that what the charioteer wants is for the object of his desire to return his love? That reciprocation

27 Translated by John Herman Merivale (1833), in Henry Thornton Wharton, *Sappho: Memoir, Text, Selected Renderings and a Literal Translation*, 59. I have chosen this translation because it demonstrates Sappho's signature form of stanzas with three long lines and one short. For a list of more contemporary translations, see Mendelsohn, "Girl Interrupted."

can be meaningful only if his beloved *chooses* to love him back. If he is *forced* to act, then what he returns is not love but feelings imposed out of obligation. Objects don't make choices.

Hence the first problem we face. We can understand the charioteer's predicament by returning to the contradiction I introduced when talking about syllabi and Beat poetry in the very beginning of the book, that of non-communication masquerading as communication. The transfer of information from acting subject to acted-upon object is not communication but mere transmission of information, to which the acted-upon object—by its very nature as an object—cannot reply. If the beloved is reduced to the status of an object, the lover cannot speak with the beloved any more than they can speak with an inert lump of mud. Objects don't speak.

It's no coincidence that this idea of transmission has dominated communication research since the 1940s. It shaped some of the most influential models, such as the sender-message-receiver model developed in the 1940s by Claude Shannon and popularized by Warren Weaver—both electrical engineers seeking, among other things, to improve transmission over long-distance telephone lines.[28] Decades later, cultural studies theorist James Carey argued that transmission in this model was for the purpose of "control of distance and people."[29] Transmission in this sense made the spread of religion possible, as well as the frequently parallel spread of empire, underpinning many of the forms of domination that colonialism engendered.[30]

The second problem we face is that the question of reciprocated feelings still takes the lover as its point of reference. If we assume that the charioteer wants his beloved to love him back, the principal concern is still that of the charioteer. What about the beloved?

28 C. E. Shannon, "A Mathematical Theory of Communication"; Warren Weaver, "The Mathematics of Communication." For an overview of this model, see Kyle Conway, *The Art of Communication in a Polarized World*, chap. 1.

29 James Carey, *Communication as Culture: Essays on Media and Society*, 13.

30 See Carey, "Space, Time, and Communications: A Tribute to Harold Innis," in *Communication and Culture*, 109–32.

What if he doesn't want to love the charioteer back? Here is where Sappho gives a clue about how to proceed in the indirectness of the relationship between her poem's narrator and the object of her desire. The narrator recognizes the limits of her power. They are the source of her frustration and envy of the "youth whose eyes may look on" her beloved.

That recognition is the point where Luce Irigaray, a Belgian feminist philosopher, begins in her book *I Love to You*, in which she asks how women and men, in light of the history of relations of power between them, can approach each other without one reducing the other to an object.[31] She expresses these limits by saying, "You are not the whole and I am not the whole."[32] What she's really describing is a form of negation, along the lines of what I suggest in chapter 1, except that here the valence is reversed. In chapter 1, negation took the form of the feeling of disorientation we feel when confronted with a text we don't understand. Here it takes the opposite form: it is what makes meaningful communication—where one person does not transform the other into an object—possible.

The path to meaningful communication is paradoxical, like so much of the argument in this book. It's communication masquerading as non-communication: it's non-transmission that opens a space for a more meaningful form of sharing. It is based on a notion of recognition where the statement "I recognize you," by Irigaray's account, "signifies that you are different from me, that I cannot identify myself

---

31 I want to note here an important critique of Irigaray with respect to the way she organizes her analysis. Throughout *I Love to You* she relies on an essentialized biological definition of sex and gender that risks undoing the very argument she is making. Her essentialism seems to establish a proper (and by extension, improper) way of being man or woman, a structure that reproduces the very relationships of domination she is critiquing. Her argument can be made consistent with itself—indeed, this is my approach here—if it allows for the same freedom from predefined roles within the gender categories on which she relies, a freedom that calls her essentialism into question. What becomes important, if we take this approach, are the relationships of domination, rather than the categories themselves. These relationships are my concern in this section.

32 Luce Irigaray, *I Love to You: Sketch for a Felicity Within History*, 103.

(with) nor master your becoming. I will never be your master. And it's this negative that enables me to go towards you" because it's in that recognition—me of you and you of me—that we become acting subjects.[33]

What might such recognition and movement look like? Since the point is to avoid a situation where one person turns the other into an object, the relationship must be "founded upon a form of indirection or intransitivity."[34] Irigaray proposes to look for an answer in grammar, in the distinction between a *direct* object—the thing that receives the action of the verb—and an *indirect* object—a thing that is affected by the verb, but not in a direct sense:

> I give a book (direct object) to you (indirect object).
> I ask you (indirect object) a question (direct object).
> She gave me (indirect object) a gift (direct object).

To avoid reducing the beloved to an acted-upon object, Irigaray, like Sappho's narrator, proposes a new grammar for love: not "I love you" but "I love *to* you."[35]

Her turn to grammar is heuristic in that it is not an answer in itself but instead gives clues about how to arrive at an answer. It is also only the first step. "I love you" turns you into a direct object, both syntactically and philosophically. In contrast, "I love to you" knocks us off balance with its awkward syntax, but, Irigaray shows, it can be dangerous, too. An indirect object is still an object, like the narrator's beloved in Sappho's poem. What matters is how I act upon this indirectness. If, on the one hand, I orbit around you, I place us both in a position where our actions are not entirely our own: you, because you are an object, and me, because I define myself through you (that is, I take you as my point of reference). If, on the other

---

33 Irigaray, *I Love to You*, 104.

34 Irigaray, *I Love to You*, 102.

35 In the original French, "J'aime à toi" instead of "je t'aime." Luce Irigaray, *J'aime à toi: Esquisse d'une félicité dans l'histoire.*

hand, I insist on our mutual finitude—the fact that we remain distinct and independent (Irigaray's word is "irreducible"), even as we exist in relation to each other—then we maintain the reciprocity or mutual recognition that makes our exchange something other than mere transmission.[36]

Something unexpected happens here. If transmission takes the form of a signal I send directly to you, then what is non-transmission? It is no signal at all. It is silence that makes it possible for me to listen: "Listening to you . . . requires that I make myself available, that I be once more and always capable of silence."[37] This is the point where negation takes on a positive valence. My silence—my decision not to speak—allows me to reach out to you. If you listen to me in the same way, we can realize the conditions of possibility for establishing the grounds—particular to you and to me—on which to build a relationship where neither you nor I turn the other into an object.

But there's more. Because our efforts not to turn each other into an object are mutual, we both stand to benefit in ways that fall outside the logic of instrumentalization we're looking to undo. The truth is that I cannot see myself the way that you, looking at me from the outside, can see me. You cannot know me definitively, "but you know something of my appearance. You can perceive the directions and dimensions of my intentionality. You cannot know who I am but you can help me to be by perceiving that in me which escapes me, my fidelity or infidelity to myself."[38] In simpler terms, think of the things you can see that I cannot. Physically, for instance, you can walk behind me, and you can see me from far away. I can do neither of these things. Similarly, you have a perspective on the way I think or act that I cannot gain without help because I can never get outside of my own mind. This is true especially if you listen in the radical way Irigaray suggests—like you mean it, so to speak.

36 Irigaray, *I Love to You*, 109–10.
37 Irigaray, *I Love to You*, 118.
38 Irigaray, *I Love to You*, 112.

In listening, I move toward you, not as I imagine you to be (such imagining would turn you into an object for me to know), but as you present yourself to me. In moving toward you, I recognize my limits, my finitude, and the fact that I cannot ever know you completely. You will always remain, at least in part, a mystery to me. But in moving toward you, I am also transformed. You help me see what I cannot see about myself. I come to see myself through your eyes (although never completely, as you recognize your limits, your finitude, and the fact that you can never know me completely, either). Whereas eros took me out of myself, in this relationship, I return to myself. It becomes, Irigaray says, "enstasy rather than ecstasy."[39]

In this way, our ongoing encounter, characterized by non-transmission, by silence, by holding back, but also by conditions in which sharing takes place between two people who strive to recognize each other as acting subjects, comes to have the form of an event, in Ricoeur's sense: it is realized temporally and in the present; it takes place in a specific place; and it allows us to say something about the world in which we meet.

The Eros of Reading

This discussion of love between people gives some sense of where I plan to go in this book's conclusion. But how does it relate to the act of reading, especially reading hard texts? Interestingly, Plato and Irigaray both relate love back to language. Plato's Socrates shows how his charioteer speech models the ideals of dialectical engagement, in contrast to the teachers of rhetoric who travelled through Greece giving performances, whom Socrates holds in contempt. Irigaray, for her part, examines gendered speech patterns and the relations of power of which they are symptomatic. But the most useful path back, I think, is through the idea of folk phenomenology, which

---

39 Irigaray, *I Love to You*, 105.

Samuel Rocha proposes as a way to understand how people come to grasp their experience of the world, even if they lack the technical vocabulary that has developed within the philosophical field of phenomenology (or the philosophy of experience). His concern is education, but his conceptual tools reveal facets of how we read, too, in ways that will lead us back to Ricoeur's concept of appropriation.

Rocha relates education back to three different modes or categories of being. They're best illustrated through examples. If we say, *The child is* _____, we're speaking of *existence*, or being embodied and taking material form. The child exists in this sense: "The child is my daughter." If we say, *Gravity is* _____, we're speaking of *subsistence*. It does not exist in the same way as a child: it's a force that is "vital, energetic, and conceptual,"[40] but doesn't have a material form the way a child does: "Gravity is all around us." The third form is the most abstract. If we ask, *How is it that something exists rather than nothing?* we're speaking of *Being*, which Rocha capitalizes (following the conventions of phenomenology) as a way to signify that we're speaking of the raw fact of being: Being encompasses all that is.[41]

It is subsistence that interests me here: eros subsists, like gravity. For Rocha, the aspect of education that subsists is study, an idea he extends well beyond its common-sense meaning. Rather than an act we undertake deliberately, such as when we read a textbook to cram for a test, study for Rocha is a driving impulse to engage with the world, a "subsistent force that allows no distinction between preparation and performance."[42] He compares study to the way master musicians work. (He himself is an immensely talented, self-taught guitarist.) They do not simply run scales and then set their instrument aside (as I did when I took piano lessons as a kid—I am *not* a master musician). Instead, their instrument becomes a medium

---

40 Rocha, *Folk Phenomenology*, 12

41 Rocha, *Folk Phenomenology*, 11–12.

42 Rocha, *Folk Phenomenology*, 84. I have removed his original italics.

through which they engage with the world. It is as if they incorporate it into their being, and it incorporates them:

> a true master of any instrument would likely describe the process [of mastery] as being possessed by something else, beyond the finitude of the person or the instrument, something not entirely physical nor anything too remote: an intense desire for rich, communal love; a genetic curiosity about melodic, rhythmic, and harmonic colors and shapes; a religious thirst for beauty and many other things that subsist.[43]

This experience translates into other domains for other people. Writing for me feels like being possessed by something else. It transports me outside of myself, even if, say, a highly ambulant virus has forced the world to slow down and severely restricted people's movement. (I am still writing this from my basement during the COVID-19 pandemic.) Rocha says, "The artist—a cooing baby, the master guitarist, a curious physicist, the passionate teacher, the tragic lover—each knows about the subsistence of erotic study."[44]

Our desire to make meaning of the world bears a lot in common with Rocha's idea of study. With the exception perhaps of nihilist philosophers, who profess the "belief that all values are baseless and that nothing can be known or communicated,"[45] most people want to

---

43 Rocha, *Folk Phenomenology*, 86.

44 Rocha, *Folk Phenomenology*, 88. Keep in mind that Rocha is speaking of eros in the same broad sense as I am.

45 Alan Pratt, "Nihilism." My claim here is more sweeping than I intend it to be. The philosopher most identified with nihilism, Friedrich Nietzsche, does not reject meaning altogether. On the contrary, he makes a forceful argument in *The Genealogy of Morals* that philosophers have misidentified the source of ideas such as good and evil used to interpret the world. He shifts focus from the idea of altruism advanced by those whom he is criticizing to the idea of *ressentiment*, or the assertion of power by the oppressed against the oppressor. The meaning he rejects relates to these older senses of good, but he does not reject meaning as such. Although I don't have the space to develop this argument further here (Pratt's encyclopedia entry on nihilism goes a long way in fleshing out this argument), even those philosophers who have followed Nietzsche's approach, such as Michel Foucault and Jacques Derrida, do not reject meaning as such. Instead they challenge long-standing ideas

find meaning in their experience. They might look for it in different places—religion, philosophy, and politics are popular choices—but they look for it all the same. Like my daughter when she was learning to read, they cannot stop themselves: everywhere they look, they see letters, and they read the words they make. Everywhere they look, they see metaphors, or texts, or most likely of all, meaningful actions, and they interpret them as best they can.

In the end, Rocha says, *"study is beyond our control."*[46] We must relinquish control as we recognize, on the one hand, our finitude and that of the world with which we engage, and on the other, the ways both we and the world spill over our limits through that very engagement. Plato, Sappho, and Irigaray have all led us to this place, and we can begin to see what Ricoeur means when he talks about appropriation, the subject of the next chapter: it is not the act of claiming a text or making it mean what we want it to mean, but of relinquishing our control over interpretation. It comes from stepping out of oneself and then stepping back in.

Conclusion: How to Read Like I Mean It

Let's return to my opening anecdote, where I read a book that excites me but unsettles me, too. The excitement I felt welling up in me as I read Shawn Wilson's book on method from an Indigenous perspective—that excitement was eros. The object of my desire was not a person, but a set of ideas so powerful that I reacted physically, reading the book until the early hours of the morning, and then finding myself unable to sleep. The ideas took the structure of

---

about the sources and nature of meaning, such as the idea that meaning derives from God, economic relations, or some other originary source. They aren't opposed to meaning so much as they are opposed to foundationalist thought. If they rejected meaning as such, I doubt they would have written their many books. Why bother, if nothing means anything?

46 Rocha, *Folk Phenomenology*, 90, original emphasis.

a metaphor, saying that A was B, or that method—the subject of the book I am writing at this very moment—was other than I had always imagined it to be. The concluding section of a chapter is not a place to introduce new ideas, so I will refrain from rehearsing Wilson's argument (although I will encourage you to read it yourself), other than to say that he establishes an epistemology (a way of knowing the world) and an axiology (a way of evaluating the ethical nature of claims we make) that deviate so far from my own that I'm still feeling a bit off-kilter. I'm disoriented and floundering, which is simultaneously frightening and exciting, as I work through the ideas he presents.

When I reacted to Wilson's book by wanting instinctively to stick up for the anthropologist whom he and his friend characterize as arrogant, I was approaching the book as the charioteer in the Phaedrus approached his beloved. Because I was so excited about the ideas, I deceived myself into thinking I was open to a perspective that was not my own. But my resistance to what Wilson was trying to tell me was a symptom of my desire to impose my own interpretation on the events he was describing. Those places where I sensed resistance in myself were precisely the places where I should have been paying closer attention.

As I've revisited Wilson's book with these ideas in mind, something unexpected has happened. I've come to ask how I might approach Wilson's text indirectly, like Sappho's narrator, Irigaray's lover, or Rocha's student engaged in study. How do I open myself to it so it can address me in the present, without imposing my past knowledge or expectations upon it? How do I meet the ideas it contains in the place they come from, rather than the place where I am? How do I hear what it has to say about the world in which we meet? In other words, how do I participate in the event of reading, in Ricoeur's sense? To do that, I must relinquish my control over the encounter. Paradoxically, even my formulation of these questions shows the degree to which I have not relinquished control, as I am presupposing the structure of my encounter with the text.

The next chapter and the conclusion will address this paradox.

4

To Read Is to Be Free

When you were a kid, what book was your favourite? Which one beckoned you to explore its world? When I was five or six, my dad read me C. S. Lewis's Narnia Chronicles, a chapter each night starting with *The Lion, the Witch, and the Wardrobe* all the way through *The Last Battle*.[1] I was drawn in by the story of four kids—Lucy, Susan, Edmund, and Peter—who, having left London for the countryside to escape the Nazi Blitz, find themselves in an old, unfamiliar house. As they explore it, they fall into another world where they discover talking animals and hear tell of a great lion, Aslan. I wanted so desperately to go to Narnia, too, to explore it for myself. In retrospect, I'm not surprised—the books are about world-making. One book, *The Magician's Nephew*, even includes a scene that still brings me to tears for its beauty—the scene where Aslan sings creation into existence.

It's not only fiction that works this way. As I never cease to mention, I am writing this book during the COVID-19 pandemic, at the beginning of which my world felt very small. I read as a means of escape when the house was quiet after everyone was in bed. I'm a

---

1 In the intervening years, the books have been reordered. They now start with *The Magician's Nephew*, whose events take place before those in *The Lion, the Witch, and the Wardrobe*. But the original order, which followed that of their publication, was formative for me.

night owl, and I enjoy the calm. I also had the time to indulge in an unusual luxury, that of reading books in their entirety, and then the books they cited, taking copious notes—more than a hundred pages by the time I was done. It was a heady experience, an unasked-for gift. I started seeing connections from essay to essay and book to book that addressed the anxiety I felt in the face of the unknown world we were entering, where we couldn't even take a walk in a park. I gave myself over to the new world that was opening up for me. I explored it, looked in its darkened nooks and crannies, felt around a bit. It surprised me in places. It was not always what I expected.

This chapter is about that process of discovery and exploration, which Ricoeur describes as a form of world disclosure, although I prefer the idea of revelation.[2] It is a paradoxical process, the inverse of the examples of non-communication masquerading as communication we considered in earlier chapters. To enter the world revealed by a text (or metaphor or meaningful action), we must first let go of our expectations about it. But by letting go, we "appropriate" the world, in Ricoeur's term: we make it our own as it reveals itself to us.

Our focus up to this point has been on the ways difficult texts are disorienting: they confuse us and force us to wander, or they fill us with vertiginous euphoria. Finally, this chapter describes how we find our bearings, having passed through these stages. It shows that to read is to be free—not in an absolute sense, but with respect to barriers that are removed as worlds are revealed. It starts by exploring this notion of bounded freedom through the metaphor of the text as a door against which we push until it yields and lets us through. Then it makes good on a promise I made in the introductory chapter. It asks how hermeneutics relates to experimental methods in the social sciences. Having shown where those methods fit within the hermeneutic mode of inquiry, it asks whether social scientific claims about how people read support the claims that I have used

---

2 Paul Ricoeur, *Hermeneutics and the Human Sciences: Essays on Language, Action and Interpretation*, 139.

to structure this book, allowing me to argue that my metaphors of reading—to read is to feel lost, to wander, to love, and finally to be free—are persuasive because they are, in fact, powerful accounts of how we make meaning of difficult texts.

Freedom Within Ever Widening Bounds

Sometimes metaphors become victims of their own success. They are compelling when they cause us to see the world in a new way, but if I am so moved by a metaphor that I repeat it to you, and you are so moved that you repeat it to your friend, and your friend is so moved that they repeat it, too, it loses its element of surprise. It becomes predictable and loses its value as a metaphor, in some cases even becoming lexicalized or turned into a word. Ricoeur, for instance, gives the example of *testa* in Latin, meaning "little pot," which becomes *tête* or "head" in French.[3] It's easy enough to think of other examples. To name one, my students will tell you (if they've paid any attention at all) that *broadcasting* used to refer to a form of seed propagation where gardeners or farmers scattered seeds indiscriminately over their fields, a sense that is mostly lost to us now.[4]

But there's value in reviving them: "the rejuvenation of all dead metaphors . . . allow[s] a new conceptual production to be grafted

---

3 Paul Ricoeur, *The Rule of Metaphor: The Creation of Meaning in Language*, 343; cf. 72.

4 For a wealth of other examples, see Émile Benveniste, *Indo-European Language and Society*, and Raymond Williams, *Keywords: A Vocabulary of Culture and Society*. We can carry this argument even further. If you look at an etymological dictionary showing the origins of words, you will see that their meanings shift over time. The new meanings have the structure of a metaphor in that they open a space between themselves and older meanings. This shift grows less apparent over time as new meanings come to appear as literal or denotative. They are lexicalized, so to speak, but their roots in metaphor always remain latent. Ricoeur, "Metaphor and Philosophical Discourse," in *Rule of Metaphor*, 303–71.

onto the metaphorical production itself."[5] That's my plan here. I want to talk about texts as doors, but outside of the clichés you might find on a greeting card you'd give to someone graduating from university, with saccharine platitudes about the worlds onto which they open. I want to talk about those doors and those worlds, but I want to make the metaphor urgent—and meaningful—again.

Here goes: texts are like doors. As thresholds, both serve a double function. First, when doors are closed, they form part of the wall, blocking our path. We must stop; we cannot simply pass through. Unless we push against them as they are designed to be pushed against (we turn the handle, we slide the door along its grooves), they push back (figure 11). Texts function in a similar way, as we have seen in the preceding chapters. They, too, push back, an action I described as a form of negation. We read texts, especially hard ones, but cannot simply impose our will upon them. We are Ebenezer Scrooge in *A Christmas Carol*, to return to chapter 1, arguing in vain with the spirits who show us what we need to see. We grasp for whatever will hold us.

We flounder at other times, too. The last chapter described the euphoria we experience as we are driven to make sense of things we read. If negation is disorienting because we feel like we have nothing to grasp, euphoria is disorienting because we have too many things to grasp. For this reason, the resistance presented by doors—and texts—is valuable. We have something to grasp, but not so many things that we feel lost. Freedom, paradoxically, depends on structure.

Providing structure is the second function of doors. They form part of the architecture of a whole house, which we can explore by using them to pass from one room to the next. Texts function in a similar way. To explain what I mean, I first want to make an important distinction between the physical world and the symbolic worlds we construct for ourselves. The physical world consists in the objects,

5 Ricoeur, *Rule of Metaphor*, 347.

Figure 11. A text is like a door: when you push against it, it pushes back. Source: Sidney Paget, *Rushed to the Door* (1892). OldBookIllustrations.com.

people, and places that surround us, which we cannot know directly, as our interaction with them is always mediated by our senses, but which we assume to exist independently of us or our perception. Symbolic worlds, on the other hand, are ones we construct from the meanings we make of the physical world. We interpret some things as causes, some as effects, and some as merely incidental, part of the backdrop that provides the context for the events in our lives. Symbolic worlds provide order that we can impose on the physical world; we navigate through them instinctively, usually without reflection, taking their apparent completeness for granted.[6]

Texts, like doors, provide structure—words arranged in a specific way, evoking ideas that, although open to interpretation, remain tethered to the words themselves. They create a new world to explore—Narnia or *Star Trek* or the world of Christmas that Scrooge discovers after his visits from the spirits. But we must open them as they are designed to be opened: just as a "push" door will not yield no matter how hard we pull, a text will not yield no matter how hard we try to force it to conform to our expectations. To enter through the door it provides, we must let go of our unreflexive certainty in what we think we know. We make the text's world our own—we "appropriate" it, in Ricoeur's term—by loosening our grip on our own symbolic world: "It is in allowing itself to be carried off towards the reference of the text that the *ego* divests itself of itself."[7]

The freedom we experience consists in the removal of barriers, not a vertiginous untethering. It is not an absolute freedom. Instead, our symbolic worlds expand and, figuratively speaking, we have more room within which to move. Although we will never have infinite space, we can always expand those worlds further, as there are always more texts to read (or metaphors to discover or actions to interpret). Our freedom is one of movement within ever-expanding bounds.

The Tether of the Text

Thus doors and texts are characterized by contradictory forces: they stop us until we learn how to open them, and then they propel us

---

6 This is the starting point for the book to which this one is a response, *The Art of Communication in a Polarized World*.

7 Ricoeur, *Hermeneutics and the Human Sciences*, 153, original emphasis.

into someplace new. The freedom they grant is meaningful because it also presents limits, even if those limits can always expand. For texts, as well as metaphors and meaningful actions (texts on smaller or larger scales), we experience this tension in the tethering effect that words or other signs have on us. In our interpretation, we can pull against the text, exploring it for new meaning, but the text pulls back. It justifies some readings but not others, and our task as readers is to demonstrate the congruence (or accuracy) and plenitude (or completeness) of our interpretation (see chapter 2).

Some checks on interpretation are contained within the text itself, but some, which we have set aside until now, are outside of it. Here we return to a broad distinction I made in the introductory chapter between a social scientific paradigm, where rigour is defined by reproducibility, and that of the humanities, where rigour is measured by persuasiveness. Although I might identify these paradigms as *social science* and *humanities*, the fundamental difference is that of their conception of rigour, so I will refer to them instead as the *reproducibility* and *persuasiveness* paradigms (see table 4).[8] I argued that social scientific work was grounded in unacknowledged ways in metaphor but also, conversely, that interpretations of metaphor and other texts could be tested against social scientific research. I turn to that task here to evaluate my metaphors about reading.

To use the criteria of reproducibility to evaluate claims made within the persuasiveness paradigm, I turn to the idea of resemblance, which

---

8 Another option would have been to identify these paradigms as *quantitative* and *qualitative*, but I have chosen not to for two reasons. First, although the categories *reproducible* and *quantitative* tend to overlap, as do *persuasive* and *qualitative*, they are not isomorphic. Put simply, quantitative research has its persuasive qualities, and some qualitative researchers strive for reproducibility (see Lawrence Leung, "Validity, Reliability, and Generalizability in Qualitative Research"). Second, because the terms *reproducible* and *persuasive* deviate from what we might expect, they force us to consider them more carefully. I have noticed that my students often use the terms *quantitative* and *qualitative* without any reflection, and I think we run the risk of taking them too much for granted. The surprise at seeing unexpected terms forces us to consider what they mean.

Table 4. Reproducibility and persuasiveness as competing conceptions of rigour

	Reproducibility	Persuasiveness
How rigour is achieved	Experimentation and falsifiability	Hermeneutic circle
What must be accounted for	Data collection: Does the researcher minimize the impact of their role as data collector? Data analysis: Does the researcher use appropriate analytical tools?	Interpretation: Does the interpreter's argument follow from the metaphor, text, or meaningful action? Relationship: What links the interpreter to the text, etc.?
Blind spots	Individual experience, metaphor	Generalizability

plays a role in both. Within the persuasiveness paradigm, resemblance is closely linked to probability. When Ricoeur argues that the most probable interpretation is the best, he is translating the Greek word εἰκός or *eikōs*, a form of the word meaning "to seem or appear" that also gives us *icon* in English. In French, he uses two words, both of which become *probable* in the English translations I am using. One is a cognate, *probable*, but the other is *vraisemblable* or "true-seeming," related to the English word *verisimilitude*.[9] The terms *eikōs* and *vraisemblable* reveal a dimension that *probable* hides, that of resemblance: an interpretation is persuasive when it presents the same image or content as that of the text.

---

9 For example, Ricoeur speaks of "le terme *to eikos*—le vraisemblable—un titre auquel pouvait prétendre l'usage public de la parole. Le genre de preuve qui convient à l'éloquence n'est pas le nécessaire mais le vraisemblable" (*La métaphore vive*, 16–17). This formulation becomes "the term *to eikos* ('the probable') a title to which the public use of speech could lay claim. The kind of proof appropriate to oratory is not the necessary but the probable" (*Rule of Metaphor*, 11). Elsewhere, Ricoeur writes, "Une interprétation ne doit pas être seulement probable, mais plus probable qu'une autre" (*Du texte à l'action: Essais d'herméneutique II*, 226), which becomes "An interpretation must not only be probable, but more probable than others" (*Hermeneutics and the Human Sciences*, 175).

With respect to the reproducibility paradigm, Karl Popper, in his influential treatise *The Logic of Scientific Discovery*, also emphasizes verisimilitude or "nearness to the truth."[10] Science, Popper says, should be testable, and to that end, scientists should be able to formulate hypotheses that are non-contradictory (that is, they cannot be true at the same time as their opposites) and that relate to the physical world (that is, they are not merely metaphysical or philosophical).[11] Scientists can achieve a description that is "near to the truth" by transforming experience—the way they encounter the world—into method, with criteria for developing and testing hypotheses.

Historically, Popper's approach challenged scientists' certainty about their findings. Where before they had sought to verify hypotheses in a definitive way, Popper showed that verification was at best provisional. Any conclusion arrived at through the formulation and testing of hypotheses, he pointed out in a well-cited example, "may always turn out to be false: no matter how many instances of white swans we may have observed, this does not justify the conclusion that all swans are white."[12] A single black swan disproves the hypothesis. For Popper, the goal was no longer verifiability but falsifiability: statements could not be proven true, but they could be proven false, and the goal of empirical science was the accumulation of evidence over time, which suggested the accuracy (or verisimilitude) of the hypothesis being tested.

We can translate this philosophical approach into a concrete method (and eventually compare it to the hermeneutic approach we have been developing) by thinking about its implementation (figure 12). Whether we're striving for reproducibility or persuasiveness, the first step is the same: we make observations. Something piques our interest, and we take a closer look. We choose tools that let us peer more carefully at those dimensions that interest us.

---

10 Karl Popper, *The Logic of Scientific Discovery*, 282.

11 Popper, *Logic of Scientific Discovery*, 16–17.

12 Popper, *Logic of Scientific Discovery*, 4.

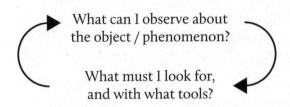

What can I observe about
the object / phenomenon?

What must I look for,
and with what tools?

Figure 12. Inquiry's first step: what can we observe, and what tools will allow us to observe more closely?

Social scientists, formulating and testing hypotheses in line with ideals of falsifiability, treat this stage as that of data gathering. For their tests to be reproducible, they need to minimize the impact of their role as data collectors, implementing methods that others can reproduce. For instance, researchers in the field of communication who treat media as stimuli that elicit measurable, predictable responses might work to generate random samples drawn from well defined groups of people. They would be explicit in how they gathered and measured people's responses, so that other researchers—drawing samples from similar groups of people, administering the same test, and using the same measurement tools to describe people's responses—would ideally arrive at similar conclusions, even if the individuals they chose were not the same.[13] As I've indicated in the figure 12, this process is circular: the tools we use reveal new things about the object we're investigating, which in turn raise new questions for which we must find new tools, and so on.

Similarly, once we've gathered evidence, we can ask two questions about it (figure 13). What does it explain, and what do we know about it? The first question, which seems self-evident, works in conjunction with the second, which requires us to step back and observe our observations, so to speak. Researchers, regardless of their paradigm, make a habit of being skeptical about their evidence. It is always possible that some unforeseen factor has influenced what they see

---

13 See, for example, Merrigan, Huston, and Johnston, *Communication Research Methods*, chaps. 7 and 8.

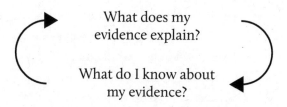

Figure 13. Inquiry's second step: what does the evidence reveal, and what do we know about the evidence?

or think they see. If they're running a survey, maybe people lied. If they're doing a content analysis, maybe their database was missing something big (but because it was their primary database, they didn't know that what it provided was incomplete). If they're doing archival research, maybe there's a miscategorized document squirrelled away somewhere that they can't find.

So what do they do? They find ways to corroborate what they have found. If their goal is reproducibility, they ask whether they have used the appropriate analytical tools. As with the process of data gathering, they want to be sure that, as far as possible, they've eliminated any influence they might exert over the analysis. They take their observations, gathered carefully and with an explicit account of their assumptions, and apply tests to decide whether they support or refute the hypothesis. (If the results of the test do not falsify their hypothesis, then they strengthen it, but only ever provisionally.) Often such tests employ inferential statistics, for example, which allow researchers to describe the likelihood that a similar test, run under similar conditions, would produce similar results.[14]

Researchers also reflect on the experiment itself to be sure that it is appropriate and that they have run it properly. They check and recheck their protocols, their instruments, and their results, which they compare to those found by others in similar situations, to see whether their interpretations are consistent. This process, too, is recursive: as they reflect on their evidence, they revise what they

---

14 See Merrigan Huston, and Johnston, *Communication Research Methods*, chap. 14.

think it explains, which in turn prompts them to seek new evidence, and so on. The question about what their evidence explains, in spite of its apparent straightforwardness, is linked to their reflection about their evidence in a relationship of mutual dependence.

Although the tools people use in pursuit of experimental reproducibility are diverse, they have blind spots, as critics working inside and outside the reproducibility paradigm have shown. Those working within it observe, for instance, that "generalizations, although perhaps statistically meaningful, have no applicability in the individual case."[15] That is, although a certain percentage of people might react in a given way to a stimulus, this fact is "at best incomplete evidence" that any given individual will react that way.[16] Similarly, reproducible analytical tools, especially statistics, strip context from the situation researchers are analyzing, leaving them, as outsiders looking in, ill-equipped to explain the meaning that members of the group make of the phenomenon they are studying.[17] Researchers from outside the reproducibility paradigm point out other shortcomings. In particular, in research about people, the tools of reproducibility tend to turn thinking, acting subjects into objects.[18] If generalizations have limited applicability to individual cases, it's because individual cases—that is, individual *people*—have the capacity for surprise. They can choose to act in unpredictable ways, although those ways might make more sense to researchers who grasp the context of a person's actions.

Going further, the models that researchers use to explain the phenomena they observe are fundamentally metaphorical.[19] Mary Hesse makes this point with respect to the natural sciences. To

15 Egon G. Guba and Yvonna S. Lincoln, "Competing Paradigms in Qualitative Research," 106.

16 Guba and Lincoln, "Competing Paradigms in Qualitative Research," 106.

17 Guba and Lincoln, "Competing Paradigms in Qualitative Research," 106.

18 Paul Willis, "Notes on Method."

19 Surely this is not a surprise. See, for example, the introduction of this book, or Ricoeur, *Rule of Metaphor*, 283–91.

say that sound is a wave, for instance, is to compare two distinct things (sound and the movement of water), and, in so doing, one can simultaneously fall short in one's explanation and go too far. What I mean is that a metaphor cannot exhaust the richness of the comparison: sound may have wave-like qualities, but those are not the only ones it has. At the same time, through the association that it creates between unlike things, metaphor changes our conception of each: the two things "are seen as more like each other; they seem to interact and adapt to one another, even to the point of invalidating their original literal descriptions if these are understood in the new, postmetaphoric sense."[20] In the case of sound, "a wave theory of sound makes sound seem more vibrant."[21] We produce meaning in the tension between the things being compared, meaning that is more slippery than scientific language strives to be.

Do these shortcomings disqualify the paradigm of reproducibility? Not at all. To understand why, let us think about how they complement the paradigm of persuasiveness, where we can apply the same strategies of observation, inquiry, and analysis (as, indeed, we have been doing throughout this book). With respect to observation and inquiry (what we can observe and what tools we need to take a closer look), we can ask whether a reader's interpretation follows from the metaphor, text, or meaningful action—whether, in short, it meets the criteria of congruence and plenitude. With respect to analysis (what our evidence explains and what we know about our evidence), we can ask what links the interpreter to the text. Understanding this link is vitally important in research about speakers and the communities to which they belong, for instance, as some observers are better positioned to interpret people's actions than others. To give myself as an example, I interpret my home country of the United States, or my home state of North Dakota, differently than my colleagues at the Canadian university where I teach because I have spent my life

<hr>

20 Mary B. Hesse, "The Explanatory Function of Metaphor," 163.
21 Hesse, "The Explanatory Function of Metaphor," 167.

participating in the communities that reside there. My insight is not without its flaws, however, as I struggle to be objective, and my Canadian colleagues often see things that I miss because I am too close. Here, too, the questions implied in these strategies are recursive: as we make observations, choose and apply tools, and interpret our results, we must constantly return to prior stages, as our results point us to new places to make observations, beginning the circuit again.

Indeed, here is where the reproducibility and persuasiveness paradigms intersect. One source of observations we can use to make and validate interpretive guesses comes from the results of reproducible research.[22] As we'll see in the next section, for example, we can take research about how people read that has been generated within a paradigm of reproducibility and use it to evaluate my interpretive argument in this book. We cannot, however, take the results of reproducible research at face value any more than we can take my metaphors at face value. Instead, we must ask what we know about the evidence used by reproducible research. What does it reveal or hide? And because the questions about observation and analysis are recursive, the stages of observation and analysis are recursive, too (figure 14). We must perform each of these steps again and again, recognizing how the answers to questions at one stage shape the questions we ask in the next, in ways that continually sharpen our analysis.

We're dealing here with a hermeneutic circle, a back-and-forth mode of interpretation that involves reading the parts of a text in the context of the whole and vice versa. Friedrich Schleiermacher, the eighteenth-century theologian I mentioned in chapter 2, describes a hermeneutic circle this way:

> Complete knowledge always involves an apparent circle to which
> it belongs, that each part can be understood only out of the
> whole to which it belongs, and vice versa. Also, within each given
> text, its parts can only be understood in terms of the whole, and

---

22 Such research helps overcome a weakness of the persuasiveness paradigm, namely the challenge of demonstrating the generalizability of interpretive results.

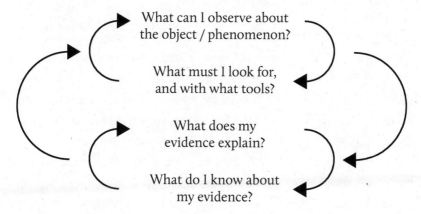

Figure 14. The recursive mode of inquiry as a hermeneutic circle

so the interpreter must gain an overview of the work by cursory reading before undertaking a more careful interpretation.[23]

What I'm suggesting here specifies the steps involved. It also shows how, by using different types of evidence to demonstrate the congruence and plenitude of our interpretation of a text, we come to a better understanding of the categories of congruence and plenitude themselves: they operate in dialogue with a variety of types of evidence, linked together in a recursive mode of inquiry.

Ricoeur gives us yet another way to think of this hermeneutic circle. For him, the back-and-forth motion is not between a text and its parts, but between the reader and the text: readers come to understand themselves by letting "the work and its world enlarge the horizon of understanding" they have of themselves.[24] They relinquish the control they would exercise over the world as they understand it and, in return, a new world—that of the text— opens up.

---

23 Friedrich D. E. Schleiermacher, "General Hermeneutics," 84–85. For the evolution of the idea of the hermeneutic circle, see Kurt Mueller-Vollmer, "Language, Mind, and Artifact: An Outline of Hermeneutic Theory Since the Enlightenment."

24 Ricoeur, *Hermeneutics and the Human Sciences*, 140.

Metacognition and Experimental Research About Reading

Let us consider a concrete example, that of research about how to read hard texts. This research is vast, so much so, in fact, that it would be an act of hubris to try to describe it exhaustively.[25] Instead, I want to describe it in broad strokes before focusing on research about one specific approach teachers have used with students.

Much of this research focuses on metacognition, or the ways we think about thinking as we read. For instance, one way to help students learn to read difficult texts is reciprocal reading, involving teachers who discuss texts with students, "questioning, summarizing, clarifying, and predicting" what an author says.[26] Another is the SOAR method, which involves *selecting* ideas from a text, *organizing* them, *associating* them (or drawing connections), and *regulating* one's learning (or practising the skills one has acquired).[27] I want to focus here on a method called SQ3R, a name that refers to its five components: *survey, question, read, recite,* and *review*. Developed by Francis Robinson in the 1940s, it is "the grandfather of study strategies."[28] Like those mentioned above, it focuses on metacognition, and its influence is difficult to overstate: even researchers who do not mention it specifically make similar recommendations, prompting students to formulate questions to guide their reading, to scan for

---

25 For a pithy summary, see Commission on Reading of the National Council of Teachers of English, "On Reading, Learning to Read, and Effective Reading Instruction: An Overview of What We Know and How We Know It." For an in-depth summary, see Marjorie Y. Lipson and Karen K. Wixson, *Assessment and Instruction of Reading and Writing Difficulties: An Interactive Approach*. In addition, in this book's preface I discuss a genre of "how to read" books published since the 1940s, which address similar themes but not from within the reproducibility paradigm.

26 Peter E. Doolittle, David Hicks, Cheri F. Triplette, William Dee Nichols, and Carl A. Young. "Reciprocal Teaching for Reading Comprehension in Higher Education: A Strategy for Fostering Deeper Understanding of Texts," 107.

27 Dharma Jairam, Kenneth A. Kiewra, Sarah Rogers-Kasson, Melissa Patterson-Hazley, and Kim Marxhausen, "SOAR Versus SQ3R: A Test of Two Study Systems."

28 Lipson and Wixson, *Assessment and Instruction of Reading and Writing Difficulties*, 690.

cues before they begin to read, and to reflect on what they've read once they're done.[29] Researchers have also built on SQ3R, often by increasing the number of steps, resulting in methods such as SQ10R.[30]

Robinson diagnosed a number of problems students faced, the biggest of which was that they "tend to get lost in detail and so miss the forest for the trees."[31] What he meant was that they struggled to see the relationship of individual sentences, paragraphs, and sections to an author's larger argument, a fact made clear in their "indiscriminate note-taking."[32] In the decades since, researchers have identified this problem again and again, remarking, for instance, on students' "indiscriminate, almost random use of the yellow highlighter."[33] They have also diagnosed related challenges: students struggle to recognize the structure of an author's argument, a problem that is both a cause and an effect of their failure to adapt their reading strategies to different types of texts and contexts.[34] Ultimately, they are still working to acquire an advanced skill of interpretation where they can recognize ambiguity without having to resolve it. One thing that makes certain texts difficult is that authors explore ambiguity in ways with which students are unfamiliar. Throughout their years in primary and secondary school, they've learned to apply models such as the five-paragraph essay (intro—body paragraph—body paragraph—body paragraph—conclusion), with its strictly structured format (topic sentence—thesis statement—evidence—evidence—evidence).[35] These models, when applied to difficult texts, work on the implicit assumption that the things students read have a meaning

---

29 See, for example, John C. Bean, "Helping Students Read Difficult Texts," and Carol Burnell, Jaime Wood, Monique Babin, Susan Pesznecker, and Nicole Rosevear, *The Word on College Reading and Writing.*

30 Michael F. Shaughnessy, "SQ10R."

31 Francis P. Robinson, *Effective Study*, 19.

32 Robinson, *Effective Study*, 21.

33 Bean, "Helping Students Read Difficult Texts," 135.

34 Bean, "Helping Students Read Difficult Texts," 134–37.

35 See Scott Korb, "The Soul-Crushing Student Essay."

that can be pinned down. This is not an assumption that the authors of the texts share. Hence one point of disconnect between what professors want to teach and what students expect to learn.[36]

Another important disconnect relates to *why* professors and students read. Professors see reading outside of class as a way to focus on the application of ideas in class, or to work through the ambiguity authors incorporate into their texts and, in so doing, participate in the process of meaning-making. That idea—to explore a text in ways that allow readers to come to their own understanding of it—is foreign to most students, who often treat reading instrumentally. Through experience, they learn that they can earn the same grade by reading selectively, following professors' cues about what is important by noticing what questions they ask on exams. If it's possible to achieve a desired grade efficiently, and if readings lead to confusion (due to their ambiguity) rather than new insights, why bother expending the effort necessary to read them?[37]

Hence the value of the solutions Robinson proposed in the 1940s. The purpose of the SQ3R method was to give students tools to recognize the structure of authors' arguments (in all their ambiguity) and to adapt their strategies as a result—in short, to come to see the relationship of a text's individual parts to the whole of an author's argument. The method is simple. First, students survey a text: they glance at headings, for instance, the way they might glance at a map to get the lay of the land. (A student reading this book might look at the headings I've used so far in this chapter: "Freedom Within Ever Widening Bounds," "The Tether of the Text," "Metacognition and

---

36 John Guillory, "On the Presumption of Knowing How to Read."

37 Manarin, "Why Read?" For what it's worth, I'm sympathetic to students on this point. The decision to approach reading instrumentally, if one's goal is a certain grade, is entirely rational, especially when students have other material concerns—paying rent, eating well, maintaining the social connections that are vital for their mental health. It's out of respect for their ability to make rational decisions that I am writing this book. I want to show them how to read carefully and openly, but I also want to persuade them that doing so has value.

Experimental Research About Reading," and so on.) Second, they turn those headings into questions, so as to "arouse [their] curiosity and so increase comprehension."[38] (Why freedom within bounds? What "tether"? What is metacognition?) Third, they read the text with those questions in mind, looking for answers. Fourth, they recite those answers, or, to choose language that feels less dated, they re-express the ideas they've uncovered: they close the book and, in their own words, write down answers to the questions they've posed. Finally, having repeated this process for each section of the text, they review the notes they took at the recitation/re-expression stage.

Let us return to the question of evidence within the reproducibility paradigm. Robinson cites a series of psychological experiments examining students divided into a control group (who read texts normally) and an experimental group (who employed different parts of what would become the SQ3R method). When a group of second-year students was trained to skim headings before reading, for instance, they read 24 percent faster than those receiving no such training.[39] The purpose of this experimental design was reproducibility: because the control and experimental groups shared similar sets of traits except for the one being tested, researchers attributed the differences they observed to the one experimental trait. In principle, this design would ensure that anyone running the same experiment would arrive at similar results. Although Robinson did not run these experiments himself, he used their results in both inductive and deductive ways. His approach was inductive when he gathered together the disparate results, each of which related to a part of the method he proposed, and synthesized them to arrive at SQ3R. His approach was deductive when he reorganized the findings into syllogisms, or logical *if-then* statements (*if* students skim

---

38 Robinson, *Effective Study*, 28.

39 Robinson, *Effective Study*, 18. Robinson is summarizing results from H. Y. McClusky, "An Experiment on the Influence of Preliminary Skimming on Reading."

headings, *then* they can read more efficiently), that then combined to build larger logical systems (*if* students can read more efficiently, *then* they can come to see how the parts of a text relate to the whole of an argument).

One feature of the reproducibility paradigm, of course, is that within it, results are only ever provisional. In the years since Robinson proposed the SQ3R method, it has come under closer scrutiny. The first critique to which it is subject is conceptual: it simply "does not account for every reason why a student might struggle with comprehension of an expository text."[40] More concretely, despite its origins in empirical research, it has been subject to little verification as such, and there is little evidence to suggest that SQ3R is effective. On the contrary, "students who use SQ3R often achieve no higher than students who use their preferred methods," possibly because SQ3R is "difficult for students to learn and apply."[41] Dharma Jairam and his co-authors account for these shortcomings by observing that Robinson developed SQ3R during a time when psychologists favoured "passive addition of information usually through rote learning activities like rehearsal."[42] SQ3R's popularity, according to recent researchers, thus appears to derive more from its being "considered part of the strategy canon" than from its demonstrated efficacy.[43]

In other words, what we see with respect to the ways professors have used SQ3R over time to inculcate in-depth reading habits is an application of Popper's experimental method in the social sciences. Robinson built on hypotheses that were verified, but always only provisionally. They remained—and remain—open to revision, and research in the intervening decades has drawn elements of SQ3R into question.

40 Jennifer A. Huber, "A Closer Look at SQ3R," 112.

41 Jairam et al., "SOAR Versus SQ3R," 412.

42 Jairam et al., "SOAR Versus SQ3R," 413.

43 Huber, "A Closer Look at SQ3R," 111.

Intertwined Paradigms: Reproducibility ↔ Persuasiveness

If we take a step back, we see that the paths of inquiry that people follow within the persuasiveness paradigm intertwine with those of the reproducibility paradigm, and vice versa. Imagine a scholar (me, for instance) working within the persuasiveness paradigm who asks what they can observe about reading and then finds Robinson's book or a critique of his SQ3R approach. These ideas give our scholar something new to observe, the effects of which cascade through their inquiry. What new tools should our scholar use? What does this evidence explain? What do they know about this evidence?

Consider table 5, which reworks the diagram of the hermeneutic circle we considered above. My approach in this book, which I situate within the persuasiveness paradigm, has shown that reading negates us before propelling us into a new world. If I turn to the reproducibility paradigm to look for new tools, I find the experiments Robinson cites or those that his critics conduct. There are clear points of convergence between our arguments. Narrowly speaking, SQ3R provides tools to formulate and validate guesses by re-expressing section headings as questions to guide the act of reading. Broadly speaking, SQ3R and other metacognitive approaches provide tools to relate the parts of the text to the whole of an author's argument by prompting

Table 5. What scholars within the persuasiveness paradigm learn by borrowing from the reproducibility paradigm

What does the persuasiveness paradigm reveal about reading?	Reading negates and then propels us into new worlds.
What does experimental evidence prompt researchers to see?	Experimental evidence shows how people read difficult texts.
What does this experimental evidence explain?	People who read iteratively are more efficient and have better recall.
What do I know about this evidence?	Experiments reduce reading to skill acquisition but miss the negation and propulsion.

students to consider the mechanics of authors' arguments. This, of course, is a hermeneutic circle.

Thus in the reproducibility paradigm I find evidence of dimensions of reading that I had not considered: people who read iteratively are more efficient and have better recall, an idea that supports my assertion that reading is a complex, iterative process consisting in a back-and-forth movement between the parts of a text and the whole of an argument. But, skeptic that I am, I also note the points of divergence, the most important of which relate to the instrumental terms that researchers use to define reading. Robinson, for instance, suggests that a student wants "any suggested method to help him (1) select what he is expected to know, (2) comprehend these ideas rapidly, (3) fix them in memory, and later (4) review efficiently for examinations."[44] Although he does not explicitly equate these abilities with reading, they are his focus when he talks about how students deal with a text. And it's not just Robinson. This instrumental logic is manifest in the emphasis different institutions put on measuring discrete skills. To give one example, government policymakers encourage research focusing on the acquisition of "sophisticated content knowledge, study skills, and the ability to proficiently navigate various sources of information."[45] To give another, as I wrote in the introductory chapter, my university requires me to incorporate measurable learning objectives into my course syllabi, leading me to write things like, "By the end of the course, students will be able to (1) identify and explain conflicting ways people have answered questions about communication and (2) find and use evidence to answer questions about communication."[46]

---

44 Robinson, *Effective Study*, 27. Writing in the 1940s, Robinson tacitly assumed that the generic student was male.

45 Huber, "A Closer Look at SQ3R," 108. Huber is referring to mandates given by different US states in the first decade of the twenty-first century.

46 From my syllabus for a third-year communication theory course I am teaching this semester, where our focus is on how to read theory. See Conway, *The Art of Communication in a Polarized World*, 132.

Consider what this approach blinds us to. We miss the driftlessness that comes from feeling lost, just as we miss the euphoria that comes from following our drive to find meaning in the world. These experiences are key to reading, if by reading we mean opening ourselves to the world revealed by a text. In this respect, the emphasis on proficient study skills comes at a tremendous cost. It makes us feel as if we are failing when we feel lost when the opposite is true: driftlessness is a necessary step because it puts us in a position to engage with the paradox of appropriation. For all its value, this experimental work turns people into objects rather than thinking subjects and misidentifies confusion as an obstacle to overcome, rather than as an important step in entering the world a text creates. With this in mind, I return to the first questions: what can I observe? With these new arguments in mind, what must I look for, and what tools do I need?

We can do the same exercise from the perspective of a researcher working within the reproducibility paradigm (table 6). Experimental research has shown that students acquire discrete skills through an iterative form of metacognition. But experimental researchers, like their hermeneutic counterparts, are aware of the things they cannot

Table 6. What researchers within the reproducibility paradigm learn by borrowing from the persuasiveness paradigm

What does the reproducibility paradigm reveal about reading?	People can use an iterative approach to acquire instrumental skills.
What does hermeneutic evidence prompt researchers to see?	An approach that values metaphor reveals that reading is more than a collection of instrumental tools.
What does this hermeneutic evidence explain?	The gap between the inexhaustible act of reading and the discrete tools studied by researchers invites an interpretation that opens potentially to a new world.
What do I know about this evidence?	The interpretation of metaphor cannot be generalized, but it can be defended through persuasive means.

explain. If one such researcher turns to hermeneutics, they might find that their empirical approach is founded on metaphor: by instrumentalizing discrete skills, it defines reading in terms of something else, moving "from one realm to another, non-intersecting realm,"[47] in much the same way as the communication researchers I wrote about in the introductory chapter. They might also find that metaphor is useful because it opens up new possibilities of interpretation to address dimensions of reading beyond the realm of experiment. At the same time, they would see a shortcoming in hermeneutic evidence, namely the impossibility of generalizing its conclusions, which must be defended through a mode of persuasion built on a qualitatively different warrant. Like our imagined hermeneutic scholar above, our hypothetical experimental researcher, taking this new tool into account, would return to the first questions they posed, asking, what can I observe? If I take metaphor seriously, what must I look for now, and what tools do I need?

In this way, the reproducibility and persuasiveness paradigms intertwine, each influencing the other at the point where scholars look for new evidence to build on their observations: things scholars observe within the one paradigm answer questions raised by scholars in the other. However, although they help fill each other's gaps, they do not do so completely. The need for the back-and-forth movement points to the open-endedness of both, whether in the provisional nature of experimental research or in the new worlds opened by metaphors, texts, and meaningful actions.

Conclusion: Distanciation and Appropriation Beyond the Text

As we move toward the concluding chapter, a recap is in order. In the introductory chapter, I said that we would explore metaphor's paradoxical *is not/is* structure, or the tension between the "literal

---

47 Ricoeur, *Rule of Metaphor*, 280.

is not"—metaphor's literal meaning, which is accessible but not necessarily true—and the "metaphorical *is*"—its figurative meaning, which has truth that is not easily accessible. Then we explored four metaphors answering the question "What does it mean to read?" Chapters 1 and 2 were about the "literal *is not*." If we are looking for literal meaning, difficult texts negate us: we read them at the risk of feeling confused and angry (chapter 1). And in so doing, they seem to withdraw our familiar points of reference (chapter 2). We grasp for something to hold on to. We flounder. We wander.

Chapters 3 and 4 were about the "metaphorical *is*." When we let go of our expectations, whether because we are compelled by the text (or metaphor or meaningful action) we are trying to understand or because we choose to, we experience something like euphoria where we are pushed beyond ourselves (chapter 3). But that euphoria is the inverse of the negation we explored earlier: we lose our points of reference and risk coming untethered from the text itself. That tether has been the focus of this chapter: we are bound to the text, and as much as we pull against its literal impossibilities, the text pulls back. In the tension between the "literal *is not*" and the "metaphorical *is*," we find a new space to explore. A world opens up that we can make our own precisely because we have let go—willingly or not—of the interpretive authority we thought we had. It is only by accepting that we might not know what we think we know that we can appropriate the world of the text.

Thus we have arrived here, where, as promised, I have held my metaphors up to scrutiny, my goal being to evaluate them from a perspective that I began by critiquing—a social scientific mode of inquiry modelled after the natural sciences—only to discover the degree to which it criss-crossed with my hermeneutic approach. We have identified a key oversight in the reproducibility paradigm, namely that it is built, ultimately, on metaphor. But that observation does not allow us now somehow to complete the reproducibility paradigm, as if metaphor were the missing piece we could plug into our puzzle and declare our project done. Instead, our observation of this shortcoming forces us to recognize metaphor's fundamental unresolvability, apparent in its *is not/is* structure. And that recognition should cause us to look again at my metaphors for reading. They do not exhaust what it means to read. Far from it. There are always more metaphors to answer the question, "What does it mean to read?"

This inexhaustibility of metaphor, combined with the processes of distanciation and appropriation, leads us to the concluding chapter. There is a pleasure in reading—in becoming lost and finding our ways into new worlds—that we can find also in interactions with other people. We've explored meaning-bearing phenomena at the micro-, mezzo-, and macro-scales—metaphor, text, meaningful action—and now we go one step further. How do we "read" other people—how do we encounter them and listen to what they have to tell us—in all their complex ambiguity?

Conclusion

To Read Is to Live with Other People

Now that I am reaching the end of my argument, my fear is that you will place this book on your shelf next to other books that say precious, forgettable things. My fear is that you will forget it just like the students who forget the syllabus their professor reads on the first day of class. My fear, ultimately, is that I will have fallen into the very trap I set out to avoid, that of non-communication masquerading as communication.

But you've followed me this far. What has been the point?

This question is really about the value of method and the texts to which it gives us access. If you're one of my students, this method will have instrumental value. You need to write a paper or a thesis to show what you've learned and what you can discover. Here are tools to do that. But what if you're one of the readers I can't even imagine?

Over the course of this book, we have dealt with texts of increasing scales. Metaphors, in the introduction, are small. Texts, many of which make use of metaphors, are medium-sized. Meaningful actions, many of which incorporate texts, are large. Now, to find the value in this analysis, I want to expand the scale one more time. Let us look at people, who produce metaphors, use texts, and perform meaningful actions. As I said in the introductory chapter, I want to answer a question about how we open ourselves up to the possibility that others might change our minds. We do so by reading in the broadest possible sense. To read like you mean it, in the end, is to find ways to live with other people, exploring their worlds as they explore yours.

We can do this through the texts they produce, at all the scales I mentioned. To get an idea how, I want to return briefly to ideas related to Indigenous research methods that I mentioned in chapter 3. Scholars such as Margaret Kovach, Shawn Wilson, Alannah Young Leon, and Denise Nadeau describe the ways that Indigenous approaches to research diverge from conventional (one might say "hegemonic") approaches.[1] Their key idea, relational accountability, makes the connection between research and people explicit. Research is good, they argue, only to the degree that it maintains the relational balance between researchers and the people they seek to understand.

There are important points of overlap between Indigenous methods and what we have discussed. Wilson, for instance, highlights the hermeneutic nature of Indigenous method: researchers are engaged in understanding and interpretation. "A key to [an Indigenous] way of thinking and . . . a necessary ingredient of an Indigenous epistemology," he explains, "is hermeneutics. [For reasons of relational accountability] we contextualize everything that we do, and we do that contextualization in a conscious way."[2] Like Ricoeur, who argues that an author's audience is potentially limitless (an argument I explore in chapter 1 and again at the end of this chapter), Wilson observes, "As I cannot know beforehand who will read this book, I cannot be sure of the relationships that readers might hold with me or the ideas I share."[3] In a realm shaped by relational accountability, that uncertainty presents important challenges, which Wilson overcomes in part by addressing his book to his children, building

---

1 Margaret Kovach, *Indigenous Methodologies: Characteristics, Conversations, and Contexts*; Shawn Wilson, *Research Is Ceremony: Indigenous Research Methods*; Alannah Young Leon, and Denise Nadeau, "Embodying Indigenous Resurgence: 'All Our Relations' Pedagogy."

2 Wilson, *Research Is Ceremony*, 102–3.

3 Wilson, *Research Is Ceremony*, 6.

on his relationship with them to establish a new relationship with his unknown readers.

In other instances, Wilson goes further than Ricoeur. Although both emphasize the reader's or listener's responsibility in interpreting a situation or text, Wilson says that they must suspend their judgment of what the writer or speaker says: "if reality is based upon relationships, then judgement of another's viewpoint is inconceivable. One person cannot possibly know all of the relationships that brought about another's ideas."[4] Ricoeur, in contrast, as we saw in chapters 2 and 4, says that we try to persuade others that our interpretation of a text is more likely than theirs. By his account, probability is the warrant for an argument's quality, which stands in contrast to researchers who are concerned with relational accountability, and who measure the quality of their work differently. Within Indigenous frameworks, an argument's validity is a function of a researcher's answerability to those with whom they interact.[5] They base their engagement on reciprocity rather than critique.

I admire the work of these scholars immensely, especially their emphasis on relational accountability. But I am not an Indigenous researcher, nor have I adopted their approach, as my efforts to persuade you demonstrate. It would be inappropriate for me to do so, at least right now: to respect the responsibilities of relational accountability, I would first need to learn the appropriate rules of protocol, something I have not done.[6] So why bring up Indigenous methods at all? Because, as a colleague reminded my students and me when she talked to us about her use of Indigenous methods, non-Indigenous people can look for echoes in their own community and history.[7] In that respect, the idea of relational accountability suggests ways

4 Wilson, *Research Is Ceremony*, 92. With respect to the listener's interpretive responsibility, see Kovach, *Indigenous Methodologies*, 72, 90, and 97.

5 Wilson, *Research Is Ceremony*, 57, 79, 92–94; Kovach, *Indigenous Methodologies*, 52.

6 Kovach, *Indigenous Methodologies*, 127 and 143.

7 Many thanks to Brenda Macdougall at the University of Ottawa for her insights in November 2020, when she spoke to the students in my doctoral methods seminar.

to expand the scale of our analysis: although our focus has been on texts, we must not forget that texts mediate between *people*, and in particular authors and readers. I want to shift our attention to that relationship, and in that way answer the call issued by these researchers whose work I admire. Thus in this concluding chapter I turn to one of Ricoeur's final books, *On Translation*, published in French shortly before he died and in English translation shortly thereafter. The book's central idea is that of linguistic hospitality, or the idea that we are released to a relationship of openness and discovery with others because we recognize that we can never know their language and world in a definitive way.[8] It is the key for expanding our scale of analysis, as the next sections show by moving from metaphor to text to action to people. These sections focus on Ricoeur's idea of ontological vehemence, which takes different forms depending on scale but relates in each case to the force that compels us to explore the world that opens before us. We discover, moving from point to point to point, that the processes of distanciation and appropriation present us with an appealing bargain: in exchange for a certainty that was never ours in the first place, we can have, instead, the pleasure of living with others and exploring the worlds they inhabit. Finally, I close the book by returning to a theme that opened it, namely the need for action and the challenges that we as readers and listeners face in the increasingly polarized world in which we live.

Ontological Vehemence: Metaphor, Text, Meaningful Action

The term *ontological vehemence* appears with increasing frequency in the works Ricoeur wrote at the end of his life, but it "is a tricky matter to write about," according to Paul Anthony Custer, "since it

---

8 Paul Ricoeur, *On Translation*, 10.

appears in scattered and fugitive traces in these works."[9] I would define it as the potential of a text, whatever its scale, to reveal a new world, in particular as that potential elicits a drive in readers to discover that world. It is the same drive I referred to as eros (chapter 3), that we feel in reaction to the negation we experience when we must yield to the text's obdurate nature (chapters 1 and 2). Perhaps the reason the term is compelling is that Ricoeur leaves it largely undefined. It promises to reveal something I hadn't thought of before, and I feel compelled to understand it. In that respect, it illustrates the very idea it describes.

I first spoke of ontological vehemence in the introductory chapter as a way to describe our drive to make sense of a metaphor's figurative meaning (the "metaphorical *is*"), which leads us someplace new, in the face of its impossible literal meaning (the "literal *is not*"). We can find parallels in texts of other scales (table 7). Roger Savage, for instance, sees a text's ontological vehemence in "the impact the work has on our ways of thinking, feeling, and conducting our lives."[10] In this vein, we might see an action's ontological vehemence in the actions it prompts from us by revealing a world we had not yet imagined, in the way, for instance, that we are inspired to do something when another person's actions help us see that change—and a new world—are possible.

Table 7. Ontological vehemence at the level of metaphor, text, and meaningful action

Metaphor	Text	Meaningful action
Impulse to embrace figurative meaning at cost of literal meaning	Drive to explore the world disclosed by a text	Injunction to act in response to another's actions

9 Paul Anthony Custer, "Speaking, Vehemence, and the Desire-to-Be: Ricoeur's Erotics of Being," 233.

10 Roger W. H. Savage, *Paul Ricoeur's Philosophical Anthropology as Hermeneutics of Liberation: Freedom, Justice, and the Power of Imagination*, 114.

Let me be a bit more concrete. In my Grade 12 English class, we read the *Iliad* by Homer, which tells part of the story of the decade-long Trojan war fought between the Achaeans (or Greeks) and the Trojans.[11] At first, the language seemed stilted and alienating to me. I struggled to keep the different warriors straight. I felt like I was fighting the text as much as the people that it depicted were fighting each other. But once I learned its rhythm, I came to marvel at two things. First was the plight of Achilles, the Achaean hero. He comes from immortal stock, tracing his lineage back to Zeus (or Jupiter, as he is referred to in the translation I cite here), but his emotions are intensely human. Throughout the poem he is torn between these two poles. After the death of his friend Patroclus, for instance, Achilles takes revenge on his killer, Hector, by stabbing him with a spear and dragging his body through the Achaean camp. This act of desecration, an expression of all-too-human grief, draws the wrath of the gods, including Jupiter, who sends Achilles' mother Thetis to persuade him to return Hector's body.[12] Although Achilles does not die in the *Iliad*, we know that the gods will punish him for his hubris, having been warned by dying Hector that "a day will come, when fate's decree / And angry gods shall wreak this wrong on thee."[13]

My second discovery was Homer's use of extended similes and metaphors (which take the same structure—the comparison of unlike things—even if simile uses *like* or *as* and metaphor does not). Throughout the *Iliad* he introduces elaborate images and then uses them to convey an idea that literal language is inadequate to

---

11 I'm using Alexander Pope's early eighteenth-century translation (along with his spellings) because it is widely regarded as "one of the greatest translations of any work into English" (Daniel Mendelsohn, "Englishing the Iliad: Grading Four Rival Translations"). I like that Pope's style, marked by the era in which he wrote, has an estranging quality for contemporary readers that draws our attention to the distance between its time and our own. (The translation I read in high school was Richmond Lattimore's.)

12 Homer, *The Iliad*, 475.

13 Homer, *The Iliad*, 440.

describe. Often, these images evoke an action of great scale, such as this comparison of the gathering Achaeans to a forest fire:

> As on some mountain, through the lofty grove,
> The crackling flames ascend, and blaze above;
> The fires expanding, as the winds arise,
> Shoot their long beams, and kindle half the skies:
> So from the polish'd arms, and brazen shields,
> A gleamy splendour flash'd along the fields.
> Not less their number than the embodied cranes,
> Or milk-white swans in Asius' watery plains.[14]

The descriptions that really moved me, however, were those that evoked characters' emotions. Consider Achilles' grief before the funeral pyre for Patroclus:

> As a poor father, helpless and undone,
> Mourns o'er the ashes of an only son,
> Takes a sad pleasure the last bones to burn,
> And pours in tears, ere yet they close the urn:
> So stay'd Achilles, circling round the shore,
> So watch'd the flames, till now they flame no more.[15]

At the time, I struggled to explain why I felt so moved. I was drawn into the image, which made me feel as the character felt, in ways that words like *sad* or *weary* (or, in different places, *excited* or *exultant*) could not express. Years later, I would read a study of Homer that explained, "Everything we describe as 'mental' and most of what we call 'emotional', the *Iliad* describes physiologically. . . . [People] in Homer have no 'insides' where emotions can reside. There is only laughing, crying, and so on."[16] I realized that when I read the *Iliad* in Grade 12 I was a teenage boy with feelings bigger than I had words

---

14 Homer, *The Iliad*, 35–36.

15 Homer, *The Iliad*, 454.

16 Rob Wiseman, "Metaphors Concerning Speech in Homer," 7 and 9.

to express, and this exteriorization gave me tools for understanding those feelings. My initial alienation from the poem, the result of my frustrations in trying to make it conform to my expectations about literature, transformed into a feeling of euphoria as Homer's images opened a world I had been looking for. They defied literal explanation, instead placing me in a realm beyond it, a realm I felt compelled to discover. Even if my reflections on them were maudlin or naive, in the way teenage boys can be, they were a clear response to these images'—these metaphors'—ontological vehemence.

Of course, in reacting to the *Iliad*, I was also moved by it as a whole text, especially with respect to Achilles' struggles between his human and more-than-human sides. It too possessed an ontological vehemence. But it's not the only text to have that effect on me. Shortly after graduating from high school, I moved to France for a year as an international student. While there, I took a side trip to Spain to see Pablo Picasso's *Guernica*, the mural evoking the northern Spanish town Guernica after it was bombed by the Nazis and Italian fascists in 1937 (figure 15). It shows suffering in its rawest form: a mother cradles her dead child, a soldier grasps a sword as he is trampled by a horse, all in Picasso's characteristic angular shapes. I remember walking into the room in Madrid's Reina Sofía Museum where *Guernica* is displayed, and time stopped. In its immensity—the mural filled the wall and my senses—it had an almost physical impact on me. I didn't realize how long I had stood there until my friends came back and said it was time to move on: forty-five minutes in front of one painting was enough.

What to make of this experience? How can we understand the ontological vehemence of a work of art, or of any text? In a book on the liberatory dimensions of Ricoeur's hermeneutics, Roger Savage imagines an artist faced with a situation—Picasso contemplating the scale of human suffering in Guernica, for example—that presents itself as a problem to be solved or, better, a call to be answered. The artist responds by creating their art: their work is their answer to

Figure 15. A mural depicting Picasso's painting *Guernica*, located in Guernica, Spain. Photograph: Jules Verne Times Two / julesvernex2.com / CC BY-SA 4.0. Source: Wikimedia Commons.

the call.[17] Exemplary works such as *Guernica*, "by subverting congealed conventions and established habits of thought," prompt viewers to see the world from a new perspective, in effect reconfiguring the points of reference they use to navigate through their personal and collective symbolic worlds.[18] *Guernica*, for instance, forced me to grapple with people's potential for cruelty in a way that I had always been able to contemplate from a safe distance. The plight of Achilles, to return to my earlier example, showed me new ways to understand the forces that tear us in two ways at once. Through this symbolic reconfiguration, these works opened new worlds for me or showed me new dimensions of the world I thought I already knew.

To be clear, I am not claiming that I discovered their "meaning" (as if they had only one) or, even more improbably, the intention of their creators. Instead, I'm pointing to the effect that their juxtaposition

---

17 Savage, *Paul Ricoeur's Philosophical Anthropology as Hermeneutics of Liberation*, 122–23.

18 Savage, *Paul Ricoeur's Philosophical Anthropology as Hermeneutics of Liberation*, 3.

of things belonging to different categories—human suffering and surreal representational figures in *Guernica* or human grief and god-like wrath in the *Iliad*—had on me. As I stepped into and then out of the works, I found meaning by exploring the tension between those things. This is how a work shapes us, not by establishing some one-to-one correspondence (image X is a symbol for idea Y), but through metaphor. The world that viewers appropriate is complex in ways that escape both the artist's intention and the viewers' interpretive skills. If the work can be said to communicate anything, it is the answer that the artist proposes in response to the call, which the viewer encounters and responds to in the world that the work opens up: "communicability does not lie in applying a rule to a case but in the fact that it is the case that summons the rule."[19]

We experience the text's ontological vehemence when, through the world it presents, it compels us to read further, look closer, and explore for ourselves. We can understand an action's ontological vehemence in an analogical way. Someone answering a call issued by a situation they face might respond by creating a text or work of art, but they might also respond through action that they endow with meaning. When we see and interpret their action, it might compel us to investigate further and—again—explore the implications of the action for ourselves: "For [Ricoeur], the 'effect of being drawn to follow' . . . takes hold when, in apprehending the act's fittingness in answer to the situation calling for it, we respond to the injunction articulated by the act by changing our conduct accordingly."[20] Imagine a moment where you witnessed someone do something that inspired you to act. Did it prompt you to see the world in a new way? In what way did it "leave its mark," so to speak?[21] Did it inspire you to see how a different, better world might be possible? If it did, you came to see

---

19 Ricoeur, quoted in Savage, *Paul Ricoeur's Philosophical Anthropology as Hermeneutics of Liberation*, 125.

20 Savage, *Paul Ricoeur's Philosophical Anthropology as Hermeneutics of Liberation*, 125.

21 With respect to the qualities that meaningful actions share with texts, see chapter 1.

that world through the paradoxical process of appropriation we discussed in chapter 4: the action compelled you to let go of your certainty in your own notions of the world so that they might be reconfigured.

Our analysis of this process of appropriation, from the micro-level of metaphor to the macro-level of meaningful action, has led us to a surprising place. The first half of this book was about the anxiety we feel when the texts we read (at every scale) resist our efforts to interpret them—when they're confusing or dense, or when they make us feel angry or confused. We resist them because they force us to see that the world is too complex for us to know in a definitive way. Our knowledge is always partial, in both the sense of "incomplete" and "biased." That fact gives rise to our desire to impose our understanding upon the world, as if by doing so, we could tame its complexity. This impulse is clear in fundamentalist philosophies, whether religious, political, or cultural, whose adherents try to impose their ideas through force. The harder they work, the more the cracks in their philosophy become clear. There is danger in this impulse.

But the first half of the book is also about how our certainty is always an illusion. It is not ours in the first place. What we are giving up is the *illusion* of control, not control itself. What we get in return is a new world. In that respect, the second half of this book is about a bargain we strike, not just in the sense of an exchange, but of a really great deal: we're getting something for nothing. We give up a certainty that was never even ours, and in exchange, we get the pleasure of a new world to explore.

The Meaning We Make of Other People

If you're reading this book as a way to understand method in the humanities, you have accomplished your goal. Go forth and read! You have the tools you need—claims, evidence, and warrants—to interpret texts and defend your interpretations.

But if you've come this far, I suspect that, like me, you see something more. Like me, you have an intuition that through the interactions we have with others, we get glimpses of their world, although we can never get a complete picture. Like me, you wonder, if we can gain access to the world of a *text* through appropriation, what would it mean to gain access to the world of another *person*? Through what door might we enter (figure 16)? Surely there is pleasure to be found there!

That is the question I raise in the few pages I have left. As I wrote in the introductory chapter, I conceived this book as a response to the question of how we open ourselves to others and the possibility that they might change our minds. The answer is conceptually simple, although harder to put into practice: we can try to see the world as others do, using the same tools to "read" people as we have used throughout this book. We have their statements and actions, both of which we can interpret in ways to reveal the world to which they point. In other words, they combine to become a discursive event, in the same way as metaphors, texts, and meaningful actions (chapter 1). Specifically, they exhibit these traits:

- The symbolic world to which the person's statements and actions refer is not that of the immediate physical environment.
- Their statements and meaningful actions make propositional claims (for example, that X is Y or A does B).
- Their content is fixed.
- The person's intention is distant.
- The person's audience is potentially limitless.

Let's consider each of these traits in turn. First, in contrast to a conversation where people can point to things in the space they share, the texts we have available to read—in a general sense, but also in the sense of "reading" other people—point to a different world. It is one that, in James Carey's words, "is brought into existence, is

PLATE 81.

Figure 16. What would it mean to gain access to the world of another person? Through what door might we enter? Source: David Roberts, *Entrance to the Temple of Bacchus, Baalbek* (1855). OldBookIllustrations .com.

produced, by . . . the construction, apprehension, and utilization of symbolic forms."[22] What Carey means is that we know the external world through our own perceptual lenses, which are inextricable from

22 James Carey, *Communication as Culture: Essays on Media and Society*, 20.

our understanding of how the world's component parts fit together. If we're trying to gain access to another person's world, we won't arrive at a place where we can point to it the way we can point to our physical environment. Their world, like ours, is constituted by its symbols.

As for propositional claims, people's statements and actions make them in two ways. First, there is what they *say*, and second, what they *presuppose*. In the first instance, what statements say is straightforward: it is their content. Actions become meaningful in a somewhat more complex way: they are meaningful to the degree that people interpret them, for instance when one person tries to explain why another has made one choice instead of another. ("Why did he do *that*?" you say to a friend, who answers, "I really don't know, but here's my guess . . .")

In the second instance, statements and actions reveal something about a person's symbolic world, which is to say, the way they make sense of the relationships between themselves and the objects and phenomena that surround them. They do so indirectly through what they presuppose. If I say, for instance, "The reading strategies presented in this book are valuable because they might help us avoid conflict," that statement can be true only if other unspoken statements are also true, for instance that avoiding conflict is desirable. In this way people's statements provide a glimpse into how they interpret the world, and our task as readers becomes one of translation. We are trying to express their propositional claims in a different way, transposing them to a different context and, in all likelihood, transforming them as we do.

The content of people's statements and actions is fixed in two ways, as well. In chapter 1, I remarked that a text's form is fixed when it is written, noting also that I meant *writing* in the broadest possible sense. Texts can be inscribed on a page or created electronically, but they also take a given (albeit ephemeral) form when people speak words heard by others. Not that we are limited to texts as collections of words. As with *Guernica*, they can take the form of works of art.

Broadly speaking, any collection of signs becomes a text if people interpret it. Similarly, actions take a fixed form when, as Ricoeur says, they "leave their mark."[23] For example, individual and collective actions by people in different levels of government during the COVID-19 pandemic have left their mark on societies the world over, as well as on individuals, as my frequent return to the topic of the pandemic suggests. People will debate the meaning of their actions for years to come, despite their ephemerality in time.

But the content of statements and actions is fixed in a second way, as well, in that the propositional claims that they presuppose are relatively fixed. These inferred propositions describe people's unspoken conception of the world, but, if this book has shown anything, it is that this stability is only relative: people can come to see their world reconfigured as they engage with other people and other texts.

The final traits relate to the ways that texts remain at a distance from readers. For written texts, an author's intention is out of reach because authors are usually not present when readers encounter their work. Some readers will encounter a text in situations that authors could never imagine, and authors cannot course-correct as they might in a face-to-face conversation. (Where are you as you read this? Perhaps you are a student in one of my classes. Perhaps not. You are not here as I write, and I am not there as you read. You are—*alas*—an abstraction to me, as I am to you.) In cases of geographic, temporal, or cultural distance, there is the real possibility that a text will evoke something for readers that the author did not intend, although that possibility exists even when an author and readers are close.[24]

Similarly, the texts that reveal the symbolic worlds of other people remain at a distance from us. At a micro-level, just as translators discover seemingly untranslatable elements within a text, which

---

23 Paul Ricoeur, *Hermeneutics and the Human Sciences: Essays on Language, Action and Interpretation*, 165–70.

24 See Ricoeur, "The Hermeneutical Function of Distanciation," in *Hermeneutics and the Human Sciences*, 93–106.

"are to a translation what a nail is to the sweater it catches, causing it to snag,"[25] we discover peculiarities embedded in people's statements that hint at their singular way of making sense of the world. We struggle to reconcile them with our own understanding. These "points that catch" are symptomatic of something larger. At a macrolevel, just as translators face "the presumption of non-translatability, which inhibits [them] even before [they tackle] the work,"[26] we sense that another person's symbolic world is so distinctly their own that it will be accessible to us only in approximate ways. To adopt a visual analogy: as close as we might stand to another person, we cannot occupy the exact same place, nor can we adopt their exact vantage point. The same is true of another person's figurative (rather than literal) perspective. We can never make a complete abstraction of our own interpretive lenses because we can never step so fully out of our own perspective as to see the world fully from another's point of view. In the process of translation, we distort what it is we purport to describe.[27]

In response to these forms of distanciation, we must undertake what Ricoeur describes in his book *On Translation* as "the work of mourning": we must "give up on the ideal of the perfect translation."[28] Paradoxically, this work is liberating, just like so many other dimensions of communication we have explored, in particular the process of appropriation: "it is this mourning for the absolute translation"—in our case, the idea that we could ever see someone's symbolic world as they see it, without distortion or loss—"that produces the happiness associated with translation."[29]

---

25 Kyle Conway, "The Vicissitudes of Untranslatability," 936.

26 Ricoeur, *On Translation*, 5.

27 I make an extended version of this argument in chapter 1 of *The Art of Communication in a Polarized World*.

28 Ricoeur, *On Translation*, 8.

29 Ricoeur, *On Translation*, 10.

Indeed, Ricoeur argues that the joy of translation comes not from perfection but from exchange and dialogue itself.[30] Why? Because other people possess their own ontological vehemence. They possess a truth beyond our own that we are driven to understand, fuelling our desire to translate not just for trade and other necessary forms of commerce, but to expand our world in our own language.[31] Ricoeur turns to French translation theorist Antoine Berman to illustrate this point. Berman wrote about *Bildung*, or the process by which writers in eighteenth and nineteenth century Germany used translation to enrich their language. They saw translation as a means by which to leave their language, see it from the outside, and then, through this foreign mediation, come back to it with new ideas: "This circular, cyclical, and alternating nature of *Bildung* implies in itself something like a carrying-across, an *Über-setzung*, a placing-of-oneself-beyond-oneself."[32] Likewise, we come to know ourselves better by stepping out of ourselves, travelling beyond our familiar world, and then, through the mediation of the other, coming back, our world having become a bigger place.[33]

In the process, we strike a bargain similar to the one above. We trade away something that was never ours in the first place—broadly speaking, the certainty that our conceptual tools are sufficient for describing the world, or narrowly speaking, our confidence in our ability to see the world from another's point of view, exactly as they see it—for something far more precious. We find a new experience, one filled—if you'll forgive my obstinate naivety—with wonder,

---

30 Ricoeur, *On Translation*, 10.

31 Ricoeur, *On Translation*, 21.

32 Antoine Berman, *The Experience of the Foreign: Culture and Translation in Romantic Germany*, 47. In addition to removing Berman's italics, I have altered the translation to emphasize the out-and-back motion of *Bildung*. Berman's original text reads: "*Cette nature circulaire, cyclique et alternante de la* Bildung *implique en elle-même quelque chose comme une translation, une* Uber-Setzung, *un se-poser-au-delà-de-soi.*" Berman, *L'épreuve de l'étranger: Culture et traduction dans l'Allemagne romantique*, 78.

33 See Richard Kearney, "Introduction: Ricoeur's Philosophy of Translation."

like the wonder Lawrence Ferlinghetti evokes in "I Am Waiting," the poem I imagined reading instead of a syllabus in the opening pages of this book. We are offered a gift, which Ricoeur calls *linguistic hospitality*, "where the pleasure of dwelling in the other's language is balanced by the pleasure of receiving the foreign word at home, in one's own welcoming house."[34]

Conclusion: The Turn to Action

The question remains: how do we accept this hospitality? As enticing a bargain as it might seem, it still presents risk. To admit to uncertainty—to admit that one might be wrong—is to make oneself vulnerable, especially in the climate of political polarization that we see in North America and Europe in this third decade of the twenty-first century, where anything less than absolute allegiance to one's camp's ideas risks being seen as weakness. Such polarization grows out of people's fear about the rapid changes they are experiencing, along with the precarity these changes bring about. Such fear causes people to identify strongly with their own groups and see members of other groups as threats. It also contributes to the popularity of the conspiracy theories that fracture our social narratives: as fear and uncertainty increase, so do people's tendencies to see patterns where they do not exist and to attribute agency to random actions, so as to "intensify people's moral judgments, rendering them more susceptible to extreme ideologies."[35] As people come to link their identities to their political or ideological allegiances, their feeling of risk becomes even more pronounced.[36]

---

34 Ricoeur, *On Translation*, 10.

35 Jan-Willem van Prooijen, *The Psychology of Conspiracy Theories*, 89.

36 For popular press accounts of the role of identity, see Rachel Martin, "She Resisted Getting Her Kids the Usual Vaccines. Then the Pandemic Hit"; Shrestha Singh, "I'm a First-Generation Indian American Woman. I Married into a Family of Trump Supporters"; and Max Fisher, "'Belonging Is Stronger than Facts': The Age

In other words, giving up our sense of certainty about our interpretation of the world might come at too high a cost. What pleasure is there if we feel we are in danger? We need to trust that other people are acting in good faith and will reciprocate our actions.[37] Indeed, such reciprocity is one of the fundamental ideas of hospitality, a word tracing its roots back to the Latin word *hostis*, signifying

> "the stranger insofar as he is recognized as enjoying equal rights to those of the Roman citizens." This recognition of rights implies a certain relation of reciprocity and supposes an agreement or compact. Not all non-Romans are called *hostis*. A bond of equality and reciprocity is established between this particular stranger and the citizens of Rome, a fact which may lead to a precise notion of hospitality. From this point of view *hostis* will signify "he who stands in a compensatory relationship" and this is precisely the foundation of the institution of hospitality.[38]

Thus we return again to the question I keep asking: how do we open ourselves to others and to ideas that scare us because we don't understand them? This question presupposes a value highlighted by the Indigenous scholars I referred to earlier in this chapter, namely that of our relationship with others. But to understand this value, it would seem, is beyond the scope of this book. Think of all it implies. Some people act in good faith, and some do not; moral philosophers have been asking about the reasons and consequences of these actions for a very long time.

Yet this idea of relationship issues a call to action that we cannot dismiss, lest we neglect the very relationships we value. What is its nature? On the one hand, we can work to persuade others to see

---

of Misinformation." For scholarly accounts, see Kolina Koltai, "Vaccine Information Seeking and Sharing: How Private Facebook Groups Contributed to the Anti-vaccine Movement Online," and Brendan Nyhan, "Why the Backfire Effect Does Not Explain the Durability of Political Misperceptions."

37 Kyle Conway, "Modern Hospitality."

38 Émile Benveniste, "Hospitality," chap. 7 in *Indo-European Language and Society*.

the world differently. We cannot *force* others to act in good faith, of course. To do so would itself be an act of bad faith. But we can present them with means and motivation to peer at the world from a new angle. That is the argument I pursue in my previous book whose final question prompted this book, as I write in the introductory chapter.[39]

But this is not the only way to understand action, and indeed, not the point of this book. In making my argument, from my silly scenarios in the introductory chapter to now, I have found a world that opened itself to me. The call to action I hear is much broader than that of persuading others. Instead, it is an action we undertake for ourselves. In seeing another's world, we realize the value of our relationship with them. Because of that relationship, we are called now to explore that world.

Let that be the action we undertake.

---

39 "How do we change people's minds?" I ask: "By opening ourselves to the possibility that they might change our minds, too." Conway, *The Art of Communication in a Polarized World*, 128.

References

Adler, Mortimer J. *How to Read a Book: The Art of Getting a Liberal Education.*
New York: Simon and Schuster, 1940. https://archive.org/details/
howtoreadbookartooadle.

Adler, Mortimer J., and Charles van Doren. *How to Read a Book: The Classic
Guide to Intelligent Reading.* New York: Simon and Schuster, 1972.

Alessandrini, Anthony. "Against 'Critical Thinking': Are We Giving Students
the Right Tools?" *Clarion*, December 2019. https://www.psc-cuny.org/
clarion/december-2019/against-%E2%80%98critical-thinking%E2%80
%99.

Althusser, Louis. "Ideology and Ideological State Apparatuses (Notes
Towards an Investigation)." Translated by Ben Brewster. In *Lenin and
Philosophy and Other Essays.* New York: Monthly Review Press, 1971.
E-version prepared by Andy Blunden, Marxists Internet Archive,
https://www.marxists.org/reference/archive/althusser/1970/ideology
.htm.

Arendt, Hannah. *The Human Condition.* Chicago: University of Chicago Press,
1958. https://archive.org/details/humanconditionooooaren_z9k6.

Aristotle. *On Interpretation.* Translated by E. M. Edghill. Cambridge, MA:
MIT Internet Classics Archive, 1994. http://classics.mit.edu/Aristotle/
interpretation.html.

Aristotle. *Poetics.* Edited with critical notes and a translation by S. H.
Butcher, 2nd rev. ed. London: Macmillan, 1898. https://archive.org/details/
poeticsofaristoooaris.

Aristotle. *Rhetoric.* Translated by W. Rhys Roberts. In *The Rhetoric and the
Poetics of Aristotle*, 19–218. New York: Modern Library, 1984. https://archive
.org/details/rhetoricpoetoodavi.

Austin, J. L. *How to Do Things with Words.* Cambridge, MA: Harvard University
Press, 1962. https://archive.org/details/howtodothingswithwords.

Bakhtin, M. M. *The Dialogic Imagination*. Edited by Michael Holquist, translated by Caryl Emerson and Michael Holquist. Austin: University of Texas Press, 1981.

Barthes, Roland. "Myth Today." In *Mythologies*, 109–59. Translated by Annette Lavers. New York: Hill and Wang, 1972.

Bean, John C. "Helping Students Read Difficult Texts." In *Engaging Ideas: The Professor's Guide to Integrating Writing, Critical Thinking, and Active Learning in the Classroom*, 133–48. San Francisco: Jossey-Bass, 2001.

Benveniste, Émile. *Indo-European Language and Society*. Coral Gables, FL: University of Miami Press, 1973. http://nrs.harvard.edu/urn-3:hul.ebook: CHS_Benveniste.Indo-European_Language_and_Society.1973.

Berger, Charles R., and Richard J. Calabrese. "Some Explorations in Initial Interaction and Beyond: Toward a Developmental Theory of Interpersonal Communication." *Human Communication Research* 1, no. 2 (1975): 99–112. https://doi.org/10.1111/j.1468-2958.1975.tb00258.x.

Berman, Antoine. *L'épreuve de l'étranger: Culture et traduction dans l'Allemagne romantique*. Paris: Gallimard, 1984.

Berman, Antoine. *The Experience of the Foreign: Culture and Translation in Romantic Germany*. Translated by S. Seyvaert. Albany, NY: SUNY Press, 1992.

Bloom, Harold. *How to Read and Why*. Toronto: Scribner, 2000. https://archive .org/details/howtoreadwhyoobloo_1.

Bruni, Frank. "The End of College as We Knew It?" *New York Times*, 4 June 2020.

Burke, Kenneth. "Four Master Tropes." *Kenyon Review* 3, no. 4 (1941): 421–38.

Burnell, Carol, Jaime Wood, Monique Babin, Susan Pesznecker, and Nicole Rosevear. *The Word on College Reading and Writing*. Salem: Open Oregon Educational Resources, 2020?. https://openoregon.pressbooks.pub/wrd/.

Butler, Judith. "A 'Bad Writer' Bites Back." *New York Times*, 20 March 1999. https://archive.nytimes.com/query.nytimes.com/gst/fullpage -950CE5D61531F933A15750C0A96F958260.html.

Carey, James. *Communication as Culture: Essays on Media and Society*, rev. ed. New York: Routledge, 2009. https://doi.org/10.4324/9780203928912.

Carroll, Lewis. *Alice's Adventures in Wonderland*. 1865. E-book edition prepared by Jana Srna, Emmy and the Online Distributed Proofreading Team. Salt Lake City: Project Gutenberg, 2009. http://www.gutenberg.org/ebooks/28885.

Carroll, Lewis. *Through the Looking-Glass*. 1871. E-book edition prepared by David Widger. Salt Lake City: Project Gutenberg, 1991. http://www .gutenberg.org/ebooks/12.

Chang, Briankle G. "Deconstructing Communication." In *Theorizing Communication: Readings Across Traditions*, edited by Robert T. Craig and Heidi L. Muller, 251–56. Los Angeles: Sage, 2007.

Commission on Reading of the National Council of Teachers of English. "On Reading, Learning to Read, and Effective Reading Instruction: An Overview of What We Know and How We Know It." National Council of Teachers of English, 1 May 2004. https://web.archive.org/web/20090320222858/http://www.ncte.org/positions/statements/onreading.

Conway, Kyle. *The Art of Communication in a Polarized World*. Edmonton, AB: Athabasca University Press, 2020. https://doi.org/10.15215/aupress/9781771992930.01.

Conway, Kyle. Little Mosque on the Prairie *and the Paradoxes of Cultural Translation*. Toronto: University of Toronto Press, 2017.

Conway, Kyle. "Modern Hospitality." *North Dakota Quarterly* 84, nos. 1–2 (2017): 185–94. https://ndquarterly.org/2017/08/24/kyle-conway-modern-hospitality/.

Conway, Kyle. "The Vicissitudes of Untranslatability." *Perspectives* 28, no. 6 (2020): 935–41. https://doi.org/10.1080/0907676X.2020.1766170.

Culler, Jonathan. *Literary Theory: A Very Short Introduction*. New York: Oxford University Press, 1997.

Custer, Paul Anthony. "Speaking, Vehemence, and the Desire-to-Be: Ricoeur's Erotics of Being." *Philosophy and Rhetoric* 52, no. 3 (2019): 232–46. https://doi.org/10.5325/philrhet.52.3.0232.

Dalton, Roque. "Like You." Translated by Jack Hirschman. In *Poetry Like Bread: Poets of the Political Imagination*, ed. Martín Espada. Willimantic, CT: Curbstone Press, 2000. https://poets.org/poem/you-1.

Dickens, Charles. *A Christmas Carol*. Toronto: Hodder and Stoughton, 1911. http://www.archive.org/details/christmascaroloodick.

Doolittle, Peter E., David Hicks, Cheri F. Triplette, William Dee Nichols, and Carl A. Young. "Reciprocal Teaching for Reading Comprehension in Higher Education: A Strategy for Fostering Deeper Understanding of Texts." *International Journal of Teaching and Learning in Higher Education* 17, no. 2 (2006): 106–18.

Dutton, Denis. "Language Crimes: A Lesson in How Not to Write, Courtesy of the Professoriate." *Wall Street Journal*, 5 February 1999. http://www.denisdutton.com/language_crimes.htm.

Eagleton, Terry. *Literary Theory: An Introduction*, 2nd ed. Minneapolis: University of Minnesota Press, 1996.

Edgar Budde, Mariann. "Wandering the COVID-19 Wilderness." Episcopal Diocese of Washington. 19 March 2020. https://web.archive.org/web/20200320131800/https://www.edow.org/about/bishop-mariann/writings/2020/03/19/wandering-covid-19-wilderness.

Felski, Rita. *The Limits of Critique*. Chicago: University of Chicago Press, 2015.

Ferlinghetti, Lawrence. "I Am Waiting." In *A Coney Island of the Mind*, 49–53. New York: New Directions, 1958. https://www.poetryfoundation.org/poems/42869/i-am-waiting-56d22183d718a.

Fish, Stanley. "Professor Sokal's Bad Joke." *New York Times*, 21 May 1996.

Fisher, Max. "'Belonging Is Stronger than Facts': The Age of Misinformation." *New York Times*, 7 May 2021.

García, Rodrigo. "A Letter to My Father, Gabriel García Márquez." *New York Times*, 6 May 2020.

Goldberg, Jonathan. *Sappho:]fragments*. Earth, Milky Way: punctum, 2018. https://doi.org/10.21983/P3.0238.1.00.

Guba, Egon. G., and Yvonna S. Lincoln. "Competing Paradigms in Qualitative Research." In *Handbook of Qualitative Research*, edited by Norman K. Denzin and Yvonna S. Lincoln, 105–17. Thousand Oaks, CA: Sage, 1994. https://archive.org/details/handbookofqualitoooounse_c9a5.

Guillory, John. "On the Presumption of Knowing How to Read." *ADE Bulletin* 145 (2008): 8–11. https://doi.org/10.1632/ade.145.8.

Halsema, Annemie. "Metaphor." In *Symptoms of the Planetary Condition: A Critical Vocabulary*, edited by Mercedes Bunz, Birgit Mara Kaiser, and Kathrin Thiele, 79–84. Lüneburg, Germany: Meson, 2017. https://doi.org/10.14619/018.

Harman, Graham. *Art and Objects*. London: Polity, 2019.

Heller, Kaitlin, and Suzanne Conklin Akbari, eds. *How We Read: Tales, Fury, Nothing, Sound*. Earth, Milky Way: punctum, 2019. https://doi.org/10.21983/P3.0259.1.00.

Hesse, Mary B. "The Explanatory Function of Metaphor." In *Models and Analogies in Science*, 157–77. Notre Dame, IN: University of Notre Dame Press, 1966. https://archive.org/details/modelsanalogiesioooohess.

Homer. *The Iliad*. Translated by Alexander Pope, 1715–20. New York: Oxford University Press, 1934. https://archive.org/details/in.ernet.dli.2015.239224.

Homer. *The Odyssey*. Vol. 1. Translated by A. T. Murray. Cambridge, MA: Harvard University Press, 1946. https://archive.org/details/in.ernet.dli.2015.281511.

Huber, Jennifer A. "A Closer Look at SQ3R." *Reading Improvement* 41, no. 2 (2004): 108–12.

Inglis-Arkell, Esther. "The Answer to the Most Famous Unanswerable Fantasy Riddle." *Gizmodo*, 5 January 2012. https://io9.gizmodo.com/the-answer-to -the-most-famous-unanswerable-fantasy-ridd-5872014.

Irigaray, Luce. *I Love to You: Sketch for a Felicity Within History*. Translated by Alison Martin. New York: Routledge, 1996. https://doi.org/10.4324/ 9781315865959.

Irigaray, Luce. *J'aime à toi: Esquisse d'une félicité dans l'histoire*. Paris: Grasset, 1992.

Jairam, Dharma, Kenneth A. Kiewra, Sarah Rogers-Kasson, Melissa Patterson-Hazley, and Kim Marxhausen. "SOAR Versus SQ3R: A Test of Two Study Systems." *Instructional Science* 42 (2014): 409–20. https://doi.org/10 .1007/s11251-013-9295-0.

Jamison, Leslie. "When the World Went Away, We Made a New One." *New York Times Magazine*, May 19, 2020.

Jowett, Benjamin, trans. *The Dialogues of Plato*. Vol. 1, 3rd ed. Oxford: Clarendon, 1892. https://archive.org/details/b24750189_0001/.

Junior, Nyasha. "Exodus." In *Women's Bible Commentary*, 25th anniversary ed., edited by Carol A. Newsom, Sharon H. Ringe, and Jacqueline E. Lapsley, 56–66. Louisville, KY: Westminster John Knox, 2012.

Kearney, Richard. "Introduction: Ricoeur's Philosophy of Translation." In Ricoeur, *On Translation*, vii–xx.

Keller, Evelyn Fox, Steven Fuller, Paul Boghossian, Thomas Nagel, Franco Moretti, Ellen Schrecker, Peter Caws, Teri Reynolds, David Layton, Lee Smolin, and George Levine. "The Sokal Hoax: A Forum." *Lingua Franca*, July–August 1996. http://linguafranca.mirror.theinfo.org/9607/tsh.html.

Koltai, Kolina. "Vaccine Information Seeking and Sharing: How Private Facebook Groups Contributed to the Anti-vaccine Movement Online." Selected Papers of #AoIR2020: The 21st Annual Conference of the Association of Internet Researchers, 27–31 October 2020. https://doi.org/ 10.5210/spir.v2020i0.11252.

Korb, Scott. "The Soul-Crushing Student Essay." *New York Times*, 12 April 2018.

Kovach, Margaret. *Indigenous Methodologies: Characteristics, Conversations, and Contexts*. Toronto: University of Toronto Press, 2009.

Lei, Simon A., Patricia J. Rhinehart, Holly A. Howard, and Jonathan K. Cho. "Strategies for Improving Reading Comprehension among College Students." *Reading Improvement* 47, no. 1 (2010): 30–42.

Leung, Lawrence. "Validity, Reliability, and Generalizability in Qualitative Research." *Journal of Family Medicine and Primary Care* 4, no. 3 (2015): 324–27. https://doi.org/10.4103/2249-4863.161306.

Lévi-Strauss, Claude. *Tristes Tropiques*. Translated by John Russell. New York: Criterion, 1961. https://archive.org/details/tristestropiques000177mbp.

Lezra, Jacques. *Untranslating Machines: A Genealogy for the Ends of Global Thought*. New York: Rowman and Littlefield International, 2017.

Lilla, Mark. "No One Knows What's Going to Happen." *New York Times*, 22 May 2020.

Lipson, Marjorie Y., and Karen K. Wixson. *Assessment and Instruction of Reading and Writing Difficulties: An Interactive Approach*. 4th ed. Toronto: Pearson, 2009. https://archive.org/details/assessmentinstru0000lips.

Maitland, Sarah. *What Is Cultural Translation?* New York: Bloomsbury, 2017.

Manarin, Karen. "Why Read?" *Higher Education Research and Development* 38, no. 1 (2019): 11–23. https://doi.org/10.1080/07294360.2018.1527296.

Martin, Rachel. "She Resisted Getting Her Kids the Usual Vaccines. Then the Pandemic Hit." National Public Radio, 22 January 2021. https://www .npr.org/2021/01/22/956935520/she-resisted-getting-her-kids-the-usual -vaccines-then-the-pandemic-hit.

Marx, Karl, and Friedrich Engels. *The German Ideology*. 1845. Moscow: Progress, 1968. E-version prepared by Tim Delaney and Bob Schwartz, Marx/Engels Internet Archive, https://www.marxists.org/archive/marx/ works/1845/german-ideology/index.htm.

McClusky, H. Y. "An Experiment on the Influence of Preliminary Skimming on Reading." *Journal of Educational Psychology* 25, no. 7 (1934): 521–29. https://doi.org/10.1037/h0070829.

Mendelsohn, Daniel. "Englishing the Iliad: Grading Four Rival Translations." *New Yorker*, 31 October 2011. https://www.newyorker.com/books/page -turner/englishing-the-iliad-grading-four-rival-translations.

Mendelsohn, Daniel. "Girl, Interrupted: Who Was Sappho?" *New Yorker*, 9 March 2015. https://www.newyorker.com/magazine/2015/03/16/girl -interrupted.

Merrigan, Gerianne, Carole L. Huston, and Russell Johnston. *Communication Research Methods*, Canadian ed. Don Mills, ON: Oxford University Press, 2012.

Mieszkowski, Jan. "Here Come the Prose Police." *Chronicle of Higher Education*, 11 October 2019. https://www.chronicle.com/interactives/20191011-In -Praise-of-Bad-Academic-Writing.

Moore, Ronald D., and Bryan Fuller. *Star Trek: Voyager*, "Barge of the Dead." Directed by Mike Vejar. UPN, 6 October 1999.

Mueller-Vollmer, Kurt. "Language, Mind, and Artifact: An Outline of Hermeneutic Theory Since the Enlightenment." In *The Hermeneutics Reader:*

Texts of the German Tradition from the Enlightenment to the Present, edited by Kurt Mueller-Vollmer, 1–53. New York: Continuum, 1985.

National Public Radio. "Advice for Dealing with Uncertainty, from People Who've Been There." NPR Life Kit podcast, May 4, 2020. https://www.npr .org/transcripts/849181366.

Nietzsche, Friedrich Wilhelm. *The Genealogy of Morals*. Translated by Horace B. Samuel and J. M. Kennedy. 1913. E-book version prepared by Marc D'Hooghe. Salt Lake City: Project Gutenberg, 2016. http://www .gutenberg.org/ebooks/52319.

Nyhan, Brendan. "Why the Backfire Effect Does Not Explain the Durability of Political Misperceptions." *Proceedings of the National Academy of Sciences* 118, no. 15 (2021). https://doi.org/10.1073/pnas.1912440117.

Parker-Pope, Tara. "5 Rules to Live By During a Pandemic." *New York Times*, 9 June 2020.

Peirce, Charles. "Logic as Semiotic: The Theory of Signs." In *The Philosophy of Peirce: Selected Writings*, edited by Justus Buchler, 98–119. London: Routledge, 1940. https://doi.org/10.4324/9781315822723.

Pérez, Roy (Vanta Griege @ultramaricon). "These are tips I wrote for my students my students on how to read theory in a humanities/ interdisciplinary context." Twitter, September 21, 2020. https://twitter .com/ultramaricon/status/1308099756510466049.

Peters, John Durham. *Speaking into the Air: A History of the Idea of Communication*. Chicago: University of Chicago Press, 1999.

Plato. *Phaedrus*. In Jowett, *The Dialogues of Plato*, 431–89. https://archive.org/ details/b24750189_0001/page/430/mode/2up.

Pluckrose, Helen, James A. Lindsay, and Peter Boghossian. "Academic Grievance Studies and the Corruption of Scholarship." *Areo*, 2 October 2018. https://areomagazine.com/2018/10/02/academic-grievance-studies -and-the-corruption-of-scholarship/.

Popper, Karl. *The Logic of Scientific Discovery*. 2nd ed. New York: Routledge, 2002. https://doi.org/10.4324/9780203994627.

Pratt, Alan. "Nihilism." In *Internet Encyclopedia of Philosophy*, edited by James Fieser and Bradley Dowden. 5 July 2020. https://www.iep.utm.edu/nihilism/.

Ricoeur, Paul. *Du texte à l'action: Essais d'herméneutique II*. Paris: Seuil, 1986.

Ricoeur, Paul. *Hermeneutics and the Human Sciences: Essays on Language, Action and Interpretation*. Translated and edited by John B. Thompson. Cambridge, UK: Cambridge University Press, 1981. https://doi.org/10.1017/CBO978 1316534984.

Ricoeur, Paul. *La métaphore vive*. Paris: Seuil, 1975.

Ricoeur, Paul. "Metaphor and the Main Problem of Hermeneutics." *New Literary History* 6, no. 1 (1974): 95–110. https://doi.org/10.2307/468343.

Ricoeur, Paul. *On Translation*. Translated by Eileen Brennan. New York: Routledge, 2006. https://doi.org/10.4324/9780203003831.

Ricoeur, Paul. *Philosophy, Ethics, and Politics*. Edited by Catherine Goldenstein. Translated by Kathleen Blamey. Cambridge, UK: Polity, 2020.

Ricoeur, Paul. *The Rule of Metaphor: The Creation of Meaning in Language*. Translated by Robert Czerny, Kathleen McLaughlin, and John Costello. New York: Routledge, 2003. https://doi.org/10.4324/9780203426616.

Rilke, Rainer Maria. *Der Neuen Gedichte: Anderer Teil*. 1919. E-book edition prepared by Marc D'Hooghe. Salt Lake City: Project Gutenberg, 2010. https://www.gutenberg.org/ebooks/33864.

Robbins, Bruce, and Andrew Ross. "Mystery Science Theater." *Lingua Franca*, July 1996. http://linguafranca.mirror.theinfo.org/9607/mst.html.

Robinson, Francis P. *Effective Study*. New York: Harper and Brothers, 1946. https://archive.org/details/in.ernet.dli.2015.224377.

Rocha, Samuel D. *Folk Phenomenology: Education, Study, and the Human Person*. Eugene, OR: Pickwick, 2015.

Sakenfeld, Katharine Doob. "Numbers." In *Women's Bible Commentary*, 25th anniversary ed., edited by Carol A. Newsom, Sharon H. Ringe, and Jacqueline E. Lapsley, 79–87. Louisville, KY: Westminster John Knox, 2012.

Saussure, Ferdinand de. *Cours de linguistique générale*. Paris: Payot, 1916.

Saussure, Ferdinand de. *Course in General Linguistics*. Translated by Wade Baskin. New York: Philosophical Library, 1959. https://archive.org/details/courseingenerall00saus.

Savage, Roger W. H. *Paul Ricoeur's Philosophical Anthropology as Hermeneutics of Liberation: Freedom, Justice, and the Power of Imagination*. New York: Routledge, 2021. https://doi.org/10.4324/9781003022541.

Schaechter, Rukhl. "It's 2020 and We're Wandering in the Desert Once Again." *The Forward*, 26 May 2020. https://forward.com/life/447308/its-2020-and -were-wandering-in-the-desert-once-again/.

Schleiermacher, Friedrich D. E. "General Hermeneutics." Translated by James Duke and Jack Forstman. In *The Hermeneutics Reader: Texts of the German Tradition from the Enlightenment to the Present*, edited by Kurt Mueller-Vollmer, 73–86. New York: Continuum, 1985.

Scott, Emily M. D. "Start Looking, and You'll See Roads All Over the Bible." *New York Times*, 19 July 2020.

Shannon, C. E. "A Mathematical Theory of Communication." *Bell System Technical Journal* 27 (1948): 379–423 and 623–56. https://doi.org/10.1002/j .1538-7305.1948.tb01338.x.

Shaughnessy, Michael F. "SQ1OR." *Research and Teaching in Developmental Education* 13, no. 1 (1996): 97–99.

Singh, Shrestha. "I'm a First-Generation Indian American Woman. I Married into a Family of Trump Supporters." *Huffpost*, 26 January 2021. https:// www.huffpost.com/entry/in-laws-trump-supporters-capitol-insurrection _n_600efc12c5b6f401aea69eed.

Smith, Dinitia. "When Ideas Get Lost in Bad Writing." *New York Times*, 27 February 1999.

Sokal, Alan D. "A Physicist Experiments with Cultural Studies." *Lingua Franca*, May–June 1996. http://linguafranca.mirror.theinfo.org/9605/sokal.html.

Sokal, Alan D. "Transgressing the Boundaries: An Afterword." *Philosophy and Literature* 20, no. 2 (1996): 338–44. https://doi.org/10.1353/phl.1996 .0078.

Sokal, Alan D. "Transgressing the Boundaries: Towards a Transformative Hermeneutics of Quantum Gravity." *Social Text* 46–7 (1996): 217–52. https://doi.org/10.2307/466856.

Suskind, Ron. "Doctors Are Covid's First Historians." *New York Times*, 12 June 2020.

Toulmin, Stephen. *Human Understanding: The Collective Use and Evolution of Concepts*. Princeton, CA: Princeton University Press, 1972. https://archive.org/ details/humanunderstandioooootoul.

Toulmin, Stephen, Richard Rieke, and Allan Janik. *An Introduction to Reasoning*. New York: Macmillan, 1979. https://archive.org/details/ introductiontoreootoul.

van Prooijen, Jan-Willem. *The Psychology of Conspiracy Theories*. New York: Routledge, 2018. https://doi.org/10.4324/9781315525419.

Vološinov, V. N. *Marxism and the Philosophy of Language*. 1929. Translated by Ladislav Matejka and I. R. Titunik. Cambridge, MA: Harvard University Press, 1986. https://archive.org/details/marxismphilosophoovolo.

Weaver, Warren. "The Mathematics of Communication." *Scientific American* 181, no. 1 (1949): 11–15.

Wharton, Henry Thornton. *Sappho: Memoir, Text, Selected Renderings and a Literal Translation*. New York: Brentano's, 1920. https://archive.org/details/ sapphomemoirtexoobunngoog.

Wilford, John Noble. "Homer's Sea: Wine Dark?" *New York Times*, 20 December 1983. https://www.nytimes.com/1983/12/20/science/homer-s -sea-wine-dark.html.

Williams, Raymond. *Keywords: A Vocabulary of Culture and Society*, rev. ed. New York: Oxford University Press, 1983. https://archive.org/details/ keywordsvocabulaooooowill.

Willis, Paul. "Notes on Method." In *Culture, Media, Language: Working Papers in Cultural Studies, 1972–79*, edited by Stuart Hall, Dorothy Hobson, Andrew Lowe, and Paul Willis, 76–83. New York: Routledge, 1980. https://doi.org/ 10.4324/9780203381182.

Wilson, Shawn. *Research Is Ceremony: Indigenous Research Methods*. Winnipeg, MB: Fernwood, 2008.

Wiseman, Rob. "Metaphors Concerning Speech in Homer." In *Theorizing Communication: Readings Across Traditions*, edited by Robert T. Craig and Heidi L. Muller, 7–18. Los Angeles: Sage, 2007.

Woolf, Virginia. "How Should One Read a Book?" *Yale Review* 16, no. 1 (1926). https://yalereview.yale.edu/how-should-one-read-book-0.

Young Leon, Alannah, and Denise Nadeau. "Embodying Indigenous Resurgence: 'All Our Relations' Pedagogy." In *Sharing Breath: Embodied Learning and Decolonization*, edited by Sheila Batacharya and Yuk-Lin Renita Wong, 55–82. Edmonton, AB: Athabasca University Press, 2018. https://doi.org/10.15215/aupress/9781771991919.01.

Index

Achilles (mythical figure), 138–41

Adler, Mortimer, xii–xiii

Akbari, Suzanne Conklin, xii

Althusser, Louis, 62

appropriation (in hermeneutics), 32–33, 36, 52, 102, 108, 112, 129; and control, 27, 53, 104, 142–43; and distanciation, 45–46, 130–32, 136, 148. *See also* control, illusion of; distanciation

Arendt, Hannah, 20

Aristotle, 7, 65, 69–70; and metaphor, 14–15, 17–18; *On Interpretation*, 59; *Poetics*, 14, 86; *Rhetoric*, 14–17, 65

Austin, J. L., 30n2, 37–38, 44, 65

bad academic writing, 26, 30, 38–46, 53, 58. *See also* Dutton, Dennis

Bakhtin, Mikhail, 8–9

bargains, 27, 136, 143, 149–50. *See also* certainty, illusion of; control, illusion of

Barthes, Roland, 62

Beat poetry, 4–5, 7, 97. *See also* Ferlinghetti, Lawrence

Being (phenomenological concept), 88, 90, 102. *See also* existence; phenomenology; subsistence

Berger, Charles, 23–25

Berman, Antoine, 149

Bhabha, Homi, 43

Bildung, 149

Bloom, Harold, xii–xiii

Boghossian, Peter, 42

Burns, Erin, xv, 76n39

Butler, Judith, 39, 43

Calabrese, Richard, 23–25

call to action, 150–52. *See also* ontological vehemence

Canada, 29, 88

Carey, James, 60, 97, 144–45

Carroll, Lewis: *Alice's Adventures in Wonderland*, 15–17; *Through the Looking-Glass*, 64

catalyst books, 8–10

certainty, illusion of, 23, 27, 36, 44, 112, 115, 136, 143, 149. *See also* appropriation; bargains; control, illusion of; hermeneutics

Chang, Briankle, 4–5

Christmas Carol, A (novel), 33, 46–49, 110. *See also* Dickens, Charles

Chronicles of Narnia (book series), 107

claim-evidence-warrant model, 10–13, 143. *See also* claims; evidence; warrants

claims, 9–13, 21, 25, 44, 64–74, 108–9;
ethical dimensions of, 105; propositional, 34–36, 46, 113–14, 143–47. *See
also* claim-evidence-warrant model;
evidence; warrants
communication: and failure, 4, 27, 39,
97–98, 108, 133; field of, 10–11, 23,
60, 128, 130; and linguistics, 61; and
method, 5–6, 8, 10, 29, 58; and success, 6, 27, 70, 97–98, 108, 133, 148.
See also Chang, Briankle; confusion;
negation; silence; transmission
model of communication
confusion, 6–7, 25–26, 37, 129. *See also*
driftlessness; floundering; negation
congruence, 66–67, 70, 75, 113, 119, 121.
See also hermeneutics; plenitude
conspiracy theories, 56n3, 150
control, illusion of, 27, 31, 53, 96, 104–5,
121, 143; and *Star Trek: Voyager*,
49–52. *See also* appropriation;
bargains; certainty, illusion of; floundering; hermeneutics
COVID-19, 55–56, 71, 103, 107, 147; and
the meaning of pandemic, 72–73,
76–78, 80–81
critical paradigm, 11–13, 22
Culler, Jonathan, 75
Custer, Paul Anthony, 136

Dahlen (town in North Dakota), 29
Dalton, Roque, xi
Dickens, Charles, 33, 46–50, 52–53
discourse as event, 30–32, 35–36, 53,
72–73, 101, 105, 144. *See also* texts
discovery paradigm, 11–13, 21–23, 25
distanciation (in hermeneutics), 36–38,
44, 46, 60, 130–32, 136, 148. *See also*
appropriation

doors, 108, 110–12, 144–45
driftlessness, 57, 129. *See also* confusion; floundering; negation
Dutton, Dennis, 39–40, 44. *See also* bad
academic writing

Ecclesiastes, 90
ecstasy, 87–89, 101, 103
Engels, Friedrich, 9
epistemology, 57n5, 69–70, 105
eros, 26, 57, 89–93, 101–4, 137; physical
symptoms, 92, 96. *See also* euphoria
euphoria, 37, 82, 96, 108, 110, 129, 140;
as inverse of fear, 26, 85–90, 131. *See
also* eros
evidence, 10–11, 13, 22, 116–21, 125–28,
143; Aristotle's ideas about, 65;
and five-paragraph essay, 123; and
metaphor, 25; and persuasiveness paradigm, 127–29; Popper's
ideas about, 115; and reproducibility paradigm, 127–29. *See also*
claim-evidence-warrant model;
claims; warrants
existence (phenomenological concept),
102. *See also* Being; phenomenology;
subsistence
Exodus (book in Bible), 53, 58, 76–79;
and lessons for COVID-19, 80–81.
See also Israelites wandering in the
wilderness; Numbers
experimental research, 108, 114,
117–18, 122–30. *See also* discovery
paradigm; Popper, Karl
explanation (*erklärung*), 60–67. *See also*
hermeneutics; understanding

falsifiability, 21, 69–70, 114–16. *See also*
Popper, Karl

Ferlinghetti, Lawrence, 3–4, 7, 150
"figurative *is*." *See* metaphor
five-paragraph essay, 123
floundering, 38, 44, 85, 105, 110,
    131; and COVID-19, 71; and loss of
    certainty, 48–53. *See also* confusion;
    driftlessness; negation
Fragment 31 (poem by Sappho), 26, 53,
    90, 94–96. *See also* Sappho
freedom, 27, 37, 124–25; bounded,
    108–13; and euphoria, 87
Fry, Paul, 39

García, Rodrigo, 74–75
García Márquez, Gabriel. *See* García,
    Rodrigo
gardening, 88, 109
grammar, 61, 99. *See also* Austin, J. L.;
    Irigaray, Luce
Greeks. *See* Aristotle; Homer; *Phaedrus*;
    Plato; Sappho
Guernica (town in Spain), 140–42, 146;
    painting of, 140–41
guessing. *See* hermeneutics

Harman, Graham, 6
Heller, Kaitlin, xii
hermeneutics, xv, 41, 58–60, 62, 64,
    87; and experimental methods, 108,
    129–31; and guessing, 57–58, 63,
    66–68, 71–76, 80, 120; hermeneutic
    circle, 114–15, 120–21, 127–28; and
    Indigenous method, 134; liberatory
    dimensions of, 140–41; and objective
    dimension of language, 59, 63–65;
    and ontology, 90, 142; probability,
    role of, 22, 65–71, 114, 135; and
    subjective dimension of language,
    63–64; warrants for, 65–67, 70, 75–76,

113, 119, 121. *See also* appropriation;
    congruence; explanation; metaphor;
    ontological vehemence; plenitude;
    reading instruction; Ricoeur, Paul;
    understanding
Hermes, 87
Homer, xiii; and *Iliad*, 6, 138–42; and
    Odyssey, 6–7; and similes, 138–40;
    and "wine-dark sea," 6–7, 14, 18
hospitality, 27, 136, 150–51
humanistic paradigm, 13, 21–22, 25, 60
human sciences, 38–40, 53, 69–70
Huston, Carole, 10

illocutionary force, 63. *See also* Austin,
    J. L.
Indigenous methodology, xv, 83–84,
    134–35, 151; and relational account-
    ability, 84, 134–35. *See also* Kovach,
    Margaret; Wilson, Shawn
interpretive paradigm, 11–13, 21–22
Irigaray, Luce, 85, 95, 99–101, 104–5
Israelites wandering in the wilderness,
    26, 58, 76–81

Jairam, Dharma, 126
Jameson, Fredric, 41
Jamison, Leslie, 73–74
Johnston, Russell, 10

Kovach, Margaret, 134. *See also*
    Indigenous methodology

langue (language). *See* structuralism
learning objectives, 20, 128
Lévi-Strauss, Claude, 62
Lewis, C. S., 107
Lilla, Mark, 73–74
Lindsay, James A., 42

"literal *is not*." *See* metaphor
locutionary act, 63. *See also* Austin,
J. L.

Macdougall, Brenda, xv, 135n7
Maitland, Sarah, 21–22, 25
Manarin, Karen, xii
Marx, Karl, 9
meaningful action, xiii, 32–35, 55, 68,
81, 86, 104, 119; and appropriation,
108, 113–14, 130–33, 144; as event,
53; and negation, 44; ontological
vehemence of, 136–43; pandemic as,
72; wandering in wilderness as, 80.
See also metaphor; texts
Merrigan, Gerianne, 10
metacognition, 122–25, 129. *See also*
sq3r method
metaphor, xiii–xiv, 33–36, 67–68, 72,
104–5, 112, 133, 142; and appropriation, 108, 143; Aristotle's account
of, 14–18, 70; and COVID-19, 73, 76;
and euphoria, 85–88; as event, 32, 53,
144; and guessing, 57–58; inexhaustibility of, 132; lexicalization of, 109;
"literal *is not*," 18–19, 26, 37, 38n19,
81–82, 130–31, 137; "metaphorical *is*,"
18, 26, 38n19, 81–82, 88, 130, 137; and
method, 13, 21–25; and negation, 44,
46–47; ontological vehemence of, 57,
136–37, 140; and Plato, 92; and propositional claims, 74; rejuvenation
of, 109–10; and similes, 6, 17, 138;
and social sciences, 22–25, 113–14,
118–20, 129–30; structure of, 6–7;
substitution model, 14–20; tension
model, 14–20; and validation, 63.
See also hermeneutics; meaningful
action; texts

"metaphorical *is*." *See* metaphor
method, xii, 5–6, 8, 29, 58, 83, 104–5,
133; and data analysis, 117; and data
gathering, 116; in the humanities,
12–13, 66, 143; and metaphor, 21–25;
and reading instruction, 122–28; in
the social sciences, 10–12, 102, 115.
See also critical paradigm; discovery
paradigm; hermeneutics; Indigenous methodology; interpretive
paradigm
Moses. *See* Exodus; Israelites wandering in the wilderness; Numbers
Mueller-Vollmer, Kurt, 59
music, 86, 94, 102
myth, 87

Nadeau, Denise, 134. *See also* Indigenous methodology
natural sciences, 60, 69–70, 118–19, 131
negation, 38–39, 44, 81, 98, 100, 110,
127, 137; in *A Christmas Carol*, 49; and
euphoria, 131; in *Star Trek: Voyager*,
51. *See also* confusion; driftlessness;
floundering
North Dakota, 12–13n14, 29, 119
Numbers (book in Bible), 53, 58, 76–81;
and lessons for COVID-19, 80–81. *See
also* Exodus; Israelites wandering in
the wilderness

objective dimension of language. *See*
hermeneutics
objects (grammar), 99
ontological vehemence, 19, 57, 88,
136–42, 149. *See also* call to action;
metaphor
ontology, 88
Orwell, George, 9

pandemics. *See* COVID-19

parole (speech). *See* structuralism

performance art, 9

perlocutionary act, 63. *See also* Austin,
J. L.

persuasiveness paradigm, 113–14,
119–20, 127–30

Peters, John Durham, 21, 60

Phaedrus (work by Plato), 26, 85, 90–96

phenomenology, 39, 101–2. *See also*
Being; existence; Rocha, Samuel;
subsistence

physical world, 110–15. *See also* symbolic worlds

Picasso, Pablo, 140–41

plagues. *See* Exodus

Plato, 26, 53, 85, 90–94, 101, 104. See
also *Phaedrus*

plenitude, 67, 70, 76, 113, 119, 121. *See
also* congruence; hermeneutics

Pluckrose, Helen, 42

plurivocity, 71. *See also* polysemy

political polarization, 150

polysemy, 31, 34, 61, 71. *See also* distanciation; plurivocity

Popper, Karl, 69, 115, 126

probability, 22, 65–71, 114, 135. *See also*
hermeneutics

reading instruction, 122–26. *See also*
SQ3R method

recursivity, 5, 34n9, 117, 120–21

relational accountability, 84, 134–35.
See also Indigenous methodology

religion, 76, 80, 104; in communication studies, 60, 97; in
hermeneutics, 59. *See also* Exodus;
Israelites wandering in the wilderness; Numbers

reproducibility paradigm, 113–20,
126–31. *See also* social sciences

research paradigms, 11–13. *See
also* critical paradigm; discovery
paradigm; humanistic paradigm;
Indigenous methodology; interpretive paradigm; persuasiveness
paradigm; reproducibility paradigm

Ricoeur, Paul, xi, 80, 85; and appropriation, 36, 102, 104, 112; and Aristotle,
86–87; and ecstasy, 89–90; and hermeneutics, 58–72, 90, 114, 121, 140;
and hospitality, 27, 136, 148–50; and
Indigenous methodology, 135; and
metaphor, 17–19, 22, 109; and ontological vehemence, 57, 88, 137, 142;
and text as event, 30, 34–36, 101,
105, 134, 147; and world disclosure,
108. *See also* hermeneutics

Robinson, Francis, 122–28. *See also*
reading instruction; SQ3R method

Rocha, Samuel, xv, 57, 90, 102–5

Ross, Andrew, 41

Said, Edward, 43

Sakenfeld, Katherine, 79–80

Sappho, xiii, 26, 53, 85, 90–91, 94–99,
104–5. *See also* Fragment 31

Saussure, Ferdinand de, 31n4, 61–62,
70. *See also* structuralism

Savage, Roger, 137, 140

Schleiermacher, Friedrich, 60, 120–21

Scott, George C., 47

Scott, Joan, 43

Searle, John, 63

Shannon, Claude, 97

silence, 100–101. *See also*
communication

simile, xv, 6, 17, 138. *See also* metaphor

social sciences: and bad writing, 26, 33, 39; and hermeneutics, 65, 108, 113; and metaphor, 25; method in, 10–12, 126. *See also* reproducibility paradigm

Socrates, 85, 91–94, 101

Sokal, Alan, 40–44

SQ3R method, 122–27; critiques of, 126; and SQ10R method, 123. *See also* metacognition

Star Trek: Voyager (television show), xiii, 33, 46, 50–52

Star Wars (film franchise), 9

STEM (science, technology, engineering, and math), 56

structuralism, 31n4, 61–62, 69–70. *See also* explanation; Saussure, Ferdinand de

subjective dimension of language. *See* hermeneutics

subsistence, 102–3. *See also* Being; existence; phenomenology

syllabi, 3–5, 20, 25, 27, 128, 133; poetry as, 7, 25, 97, 150

syllogisms, 125

symbolic worlds, 11, 27, 52, 110–12, 141, 144, 146. *See also* physical world

texts, 13, 21–22, 46, 105; as catalyst, 9; defining characteristics of, 34–35, 56, 59, 72, 131–32, 144–47; different scales of, xiii, 32–35, 68, 81, 85, 104, 130, 133–34, 143; difficult, xi, xiv, 8, 19, 26–27, 37–38, 44, 51–52, 98, 123; as door, 108–13; and eros, 101; euphoric, 85–86, 96; and Indigenous

methodology, 134–36; interpretation of, 36, 49, 53, 55, 60–61, 63–67, 69–71, 124–28, 143; ontological vehemence of, 136–38, 140, 142; pandemic as, 56–58, 74; as tether, 112–21; world of, 129, 144. *See also* appropriation; hermeneutics; meaningful action; metaphor

transmission model of communication, 97–98, 100–101

Twitter, xii

understanding (*verstehen*), 58, 60–67, 90, 134. *See also* explanation; hermeneutics

United States, 17n24, 56, 60, 119

van Dooren, Charles, xii–xiii

Vološinov, V. N., 9

warrants, 130, 143; definition of, 10–11; of different research paradigms, 12–13, 21, 23, 25; in hermeneutics, 65, 135. *See also* claim-evidence-warrant model; claims; evidence

Weaver, Warren, 97

Weber-Pillwax, Cora, 84. *See also* Indigenous methodology

Wilson, Shawn, 83–85, 104–5, 134–35. *See also* Indigenous methodology

wonder, 4, 7–8, 149–50

Woolf, Virginia, xii

world disclosure. *See* appropriation; Ricoeur, Paul

Young Leon, Alannah, 134. *See also* Indigenous methodology